The International Library of Sociology

THE REGIONS OF GERMANY

Founded by KARL MANNHEIM

The International Library of Sociology

URBAN AND REGIONAL SOCIOLOGY
In 13 Volumes

THE REGIONS OF GERMANY

by

ROBERT E. DICKINSON

Routledge
Taylor & Francis Group

LONDON AND NEW YORK

First published in 1945 by
Routledge

Reprinted in 1998, 2000, 2002
by Routledge
2 Park Square, Milton Park, Abingdon, Oxon, OX14 4RN
711 Third Avenue, New York, NY 10017

Transferred to Digital Printing 2007

Routledge is an imprint of the Taylor & Francis Group

First issued in paperback 2013

The publishers have made every effort to contact authors/copyright holders
of the works reprinted in *The International Library of Sociology*.
This has not been possible in every case, however, and we would
welcome correspondence from those individuals/companies
we have been unable to trace.

British Library Cataloguing in Publication Data
A CIP catalogue record for this book
is available from the British Library

The Regions of Germany
ISBN 978-0-415-17703-0 hbk
ISBN 978-0-415-86854-9 pbk
Urban and Regional Sociology: 13 Volumes
ISBN 978-0-415-17830-3
The International Library of Sociology: 274 Volumes
ISBN 978-0-415-17838-9

Publisher's Note
The publisher has gone to great lengths to ensure the quality of this
reprint but points out that some imperfections in the original
may be apparent

CONTENTS

LIST OF MAPS

INTRODUCTORY

A recent leading article in *The Times* [1] emphasizes that the rebuilding of Europe must be effected not by a patching up of existing frontiers but by building anew on the basis of the "practical necessities of modern life". A letter in *The Times* (March 3, 1944) from Mr. A. L. Rowse carries this point of view further with special reference to Germany. He urges that the new federal states into which Germany will presumably be divided should be based on the "natural provincial groupings", which he describes as "substantial entities with their own local traditions", which already exist with "their roots in the country".

Both this leading article and Mr. Rowse, reflecting, we believe, the general viewpoint, emphasize the historical aspect of the problem,[2] but its geographical character is even more fundamental. The structure of such "groupings" or regions has been the particular concern of geographers in recent years in Germany, Britain, France and the United States, and they have a substantial contribution to make to the elaboration of principles in defining the frontiers of the European States and the divisions inside them. Modern geography regards such a natural grouping, not as a mere physical unit, but as a socio-economic unit with common economic, cultural and historical associations. The principles and technique of such geographical investigation are well established, but require fuller recognition in this country.

The problem of creating a federal Germany on the basis of regional needs is one to which German scholars and statesmen have given much attention, for the revolution in the economic and social structure of Germany in the last two generations has brought into being new entities of human space relationships that have outmoded the old historical units and their numerous detached territories. In the early years of the Weimar Republic, official schemes were put forward for the creation of new States, about twelve in number, on federal principles, though they failed through the opposition of the Prussian government. These suggested divisions adhered closely to the existing political units

---

[1] "Policies for Europe", February 29, 1944.
[2] See also an article by Lord Vansittart on "The Real Way to Permanent Peace," in the *Sunday Express*, December 19, 1943.

and, as is now generally recognized by students of the problem in Germany, did not pay sufficient attention to the geographical realities of modern life. Since then a vast body of research has been undertaken, by official and semi-official bodies and by private persons, especially by geographers, on the economic, social and cultural associations, and their integration into natural provincial units. Exhaustive studies were undertaken during the Weimar régime. More recently the Nazis have encouraged such research. They have also abolished many territorial anomalies and created major units for purposes of national planning and Party organization. The Reich departments and many other nation-wide concerns also have such divisions, independent of the *Länder* and the Prussian Provinces. All these units ignore the numerous small territories that are anachronisms in the modern world.

Eleven major natural provinces, with two smaller city units, are now recognized. Several of these correspond with existing political units but only broadly. There are, however, considerable divergences from these, and, in fact, several provinces cut right across the political boundaries. Thus, for example, *Mitteldeutschland* includes the *Länder* of Saxony, Thuringia, Anhalt, part of Brunswick and the Prussian Province of Saxony south of Magdeburg. *Niedersachsen* has its nucleus in the Province of Hanover. Rhine-Main is centred on Frankfurt. Rhineland-Westphalia has its nucleus in these two provinces, but with modified boundaries. The Hansa Cities of Hamburg and Bremen, together with contiguous areas linked with them, are generally considered as separate entities. These natural provinces exist in the corporate life of Germany, and their adoption as new political units has been advocated for many years.

The aim of this short book is to portray in a series of essays the salient features of these " natural " provinces of Germany as opposed to political provinces, emphasizing the fundamental associations upon which their unity is based. The broader general conditions affecting the country as a whole have been dealt with in my Penguin Special, *The German Lebensraum*, to which the reader is referred, and only the broader and specially relevant aspects are treated here. More detailed discussion of the concept of regionalism, with specific reference to the United States, Britain, France and Germany, will be found in my forthcoming book in this series on *City, Region and Regionalism*.

The maps have been chosen to cover, in the main, Germany

as a whole, and in reading the chapters on the separate regions, reference can be made to these. Several detailed regional maps have been added to illustrate specific points.

Figures 9, 10, 11, 14, 18 and 19 are reproduced from the *Geographical Review* by permission of the American Geographical Society. Figures 12 and 16 are reproduced by permission of Penguin Books. Figures 20, 21 and 25 are reproduced from the *Géographie Universelle, Tome IV, Europe Centrale, Première Partie*, by Emm. de Martonne.

I am deeply indebted to Mr. J. N. L. Baker, Reader in Historical Geography, University of Oxford, for correcting the proofs. Unfortunately, it has not been practicable to adopt all his suggestions, and certain defects of style and exposition, due to rapid writing when one's time is more than fully occupied with official matters, have had to stand in order to ensure speedy publication.

ROBERT E. DICKINSON.

POLISH UPLANDS

B A L T I C   L O W L A N D S

P O L A N D

Legend:
- Below Sea Level
- Low Uplands
- Scarps and Low Hills
- Upper Rhine lowland

WARSAW
Lodz
Posen
Vistula
Bug
Oder
Breslau
UPPER SILESIA
Beuthen
Hindenburg
Gleiwitz
Stettin
BERLIN
Lübeck
HAMBURG
Lüneburg
LÜNEBURG
Bremen
Hanover
Brunswick
Magdebg.
Aller
Weser
Leine
Elbe
FLÄMING–LUSATIAN UPLANDS
Dessau
Halle
Leipzig
Dresden
Saale
Chemnitz
Erzgebirge
Sudetes
Plauen
BOHEMIAN PLATEAU
Brünn
VIENNA
PRAGUE
Pilsen
Linz
Inn
Danube
Bohemian For.
Thüring. For.
Harz
Werra
Rhön
Fulda
Kassel
Bielefeld
Lippe
Ems
Osnabrück
Münster
UHR
Hagen
Wuppertal
Remscheid
Solingen
Cologne
Bonn
Koblenz
Lahn
Main
Frankfurt
Wiesbaden
Mainz
Darmstadt
Würzburg
Mannheim
Nürnberg
Ludw.
Karlsruhe
Neckar
Stuttgart
Augsburg
FRANCONIAN JURA
SWAB.
SWABIAN PLATEAU
Black Forest
Harz
Od
Spess
Wog
Erfurt
20 E.G.

EAST PRUSSIA

DANZIG
Elbing

WARSAW

POLAND

Lodz

Krakau

UPPER SILESIA
Beuthen
Hindenburg
Gleiwitz
Ratibor
M. Ostrau

Posen

Pomerania

Border Prov.

Border Prov.

Silesia

Breslau
Liegnitz
Görlitz
Waldenburg

CZECHO — SLOVAK

Brünn

PRAGUE

Stettin

BERLIN
Brandenburg
Frankfurt
Kottbus

Prov. of Brandenburg

Schwerin i.
MECKLENBURG
Rostock

SCHLESWIG-HOLSTEIN
Kiel
Lübeck
HAMBURG
Bremerhaven
Bremen
Lüneburg

Pilsen

Dresden
Meissen
Leipzig
Halle
Chemnitz
Zwickau
Plauen
Gera

SAXONY

Prov. S. of ANHALT
Magdeburg
Dessau

THURINGIA
Weimar
Erfurt
Jena
Gotha
Eisenach

BAVARIA

Upper Palatinate
Regensburg
Nürnberg
Bamberg
Würzburg

Franconia

HANOVER
Hannover
BRUNSWICK
Brunswick
Hildesheim

WESTPHALIA
Osnabrück
Münster
Bielefeld
Hamm
Hagen
Wuppertal
Remscheid
Solingen
M. Gladbach
Cologne
Bonn

RUHR

OLDENBURG

LIPPE

Kassel

NASSAU
Frankfurt

HESSE
Koblenz
Wiesbaden
Mainz
Worms
Mannheim
Ludwigshafen
Heidelberg
Heilbronn

Palatinate

Trier

WÜRTTEMBERG
Stuttgart
Pforzheim
Karlsruhe

Strasbourg

50
100

CHAPTER I

REGIONALISM IN GERMANY

I

It is widely held that one of our principal war aims is the destruction of Prussianism and the dismemberment (or " splitting up " as it is popularly called) of the Reich. This view demands a thorough understanding of the structure and needs of German society if its application is to have enduring results. For German scholars themselves have been contending with precisely this problem for many years, and especially since the formation of the Weimar Republic. The Reich is dominated in area, population, and policy, by Prussia. The boundaries of the German states and the Prussian provinces often show no relation to modern social and economic associations. From these two basic facts arises the need for a form of federalism in the Reich based upon the existing homogeneous units of human associations. This is the essence of what is called Regionalism and German thinkers have striven hard to solve it. The problem was in the forefront of the programme of the National Assembly of the Weimar Republic in 1919, but its deliberations came almost to nought, except for stimulating much research in the inter-war period, as well as giving rise to many fantastic schemes of territorial reorganization put out by both public and private authorities. The Nazis, through their totalitarian powers, have made important steps on these lines. The idea of the dismemberment of the Reich on a federal principle is nothing new. It is something for which German statesmen have been striving for many years, and which the Nazis in their peculiar way are carrying into effect, at the expense, however, of all semblance of genuine democratic government. This aspect of the matter should figure large and loud in our propaganda, for the United Nations' war aim closely tallies with the aims of old standing of many German scholars and statesmen.

The problem of Regionalism in Germany is far more complicated than in France or Britain, for it is tied up with the tremendous problems of the political reorganization of the Reich, in the government of which Prussia has always been the dominant partner. The term Regionalism is not used in

Germany ; its nearest equivalent, expressing the particular aspect of the German problem, is *Neugliederung*. The problem, however, of establishing new political divisions and a clear-cut machinery of government within the Reich, gives rise to all the same issues. In essence, the problem is to establish a group of federal states or provinces within the framework of a central government in Berlin. This problem is made very complex owing to the dualism of government as between that of the Reich and that of its dominant partner, Prussia, which covers 60 per cent. of the area of the Reich and includes 60 per cent. of its population. Ideally, the Reich should be divided into independent political units and the dualism at the centre abolished. This would mean abolishing the identity of Prussia as a state and raising its component provinces to the same political level as the old states of the south. It is generally agreed in Germany that such provinces are needed ; it is not agreed what the status of Prussia should be.

The other side of the problem is the necessity for creating new large provinces in such a way that they could serve as effective units of government. The exisiting political pattern is a legacy of the past. (Fig. 2.) In 1933 there were seventeen *Länder*—formerly called Free States (*Frei Staaten*). Prussia has fourteen divisions, including the city of Berlin and the small outlying province of Hohenzollern in the heart of Wurtemberg. The average area of each of the remaining provinces is about 25,000 square kilometres with a population of 3 millions. The other states range from Bavaria with 78,000 square kilometres and 8·3 million inhabitants to Schaumburg-Lippe with 340 square kilometres and 54,000 inhabitants. Among them are also the free cities of Lübeck, Bremen and Hamburg.[1] These States and Provinces have many detached outlying pieces of territory situated in a State from whose local government they are independent, but with which they have the closest social and economic associations. Some of these small territories are States in themselves and have long had the apparatus and authority of an independent government.

During the past hundred years Germany has undergone a revolution in its economic and social structure, and the geographical distributions of human activities and space relationships cut right across these medieval frontiers which impose ridiculous and harmful restrictions on the free development of

---

[1] Lübeck was deprived of this traditional status by a Nazi decree in 1937 and absorbed into the province of Schleswig. See p. 141.

these relationships. Thus, it is necessary that new political provinces be established, and that these provinces, in order to be effective units of human activity, government and administration, should be so defined as to combine a maximum of social and economic interest, although at the same time respecting, wherever possible, the existing political boundaries—for the problem of establishing the basis and machinery of the new government is far greater and far more urgent than that of defining entirely new boundaries throughout the Reich. Such is the problem. It came to the front of the programme of the National Assembly at Weimar, but was shelved. It has been given much attention by government authorities and by scholars during the inter-war period. Theories and facts bearing on it have given rise to a large literature which has carried the scientific analysis of the patterns of geographical or space relationships much further than in any other country. Abortive attempts were made to recast the major political divisions in accordance with the Weimar constitution of 1919. In the early 'twenties general schemes for a new division of the Reich were put forward, without, however, an adequate basis of fact. In the following years numerous public authorities and scholars published elaborate investigations of the various aspects of the general problem and of particular regions. Important regroupings of administrative areas were effected under the Weimar régime. The Nazis have also removed some of the old territorial anomalies which have been matters of bitter contention for many years—notably the creation of a single administrative authority at Hamburg, and the elimination of the many small outliers of territory between Lübeck and Hamburg and along the Mecklenburg border. They have established a new framework of administrative regions for regional planning and party organization, following the principles we have suggested. They have standardized the administration throughout the Reich and standardized the status of the *Länder* by depriving them of their rights of democratic self-government. They are working towards a solution of the problem of Regionalism in Germany, though it would appear to be the very antithesis of the democratic ideal envisaged by the United Nations.

The problem of the territorial reorganization of the Reich is one of combining the organs of government of Prussia, the dominant State, with that of the Reich, and of establishing the provinces of Prussia on the same level as the old States of the south ; and, in the process of territorial reorganization, to abolish the numerous outliers and inliers of territory. But these existing divisions are of various sizes with various population totals, and are, in fact, in their present outline, of relatively recent origin. (Fig. 2.) The largest are the States of south Germany—Bavaria, Wurtemberg, and Baden ; the States of central Germany—Saxony, Thuringia, and Hesse ; all the Prussian provinces west of the Elbe—Saxony, Hesse-Nassau, Rhineland, Westphalia and Hanover. Each of these corresponds with the type of new unit that is generally envisaged. This also applies to the Prussian provinces east of the Elbe—Brandenburg, Pomerania, East Prussia and Silesia. Entirely different States (*Länder*) are, however, the remnants of the old historical units—Oldenburg, Brunswick, Anhalt, Waldeck (absorbed by Prussia in 1929), the two Lippe states, the two Mecklenburgs (united in 1934), and (until 1920) the Thuringian states. There are also many small territories, which like the small states, have no place in the economy and administration of the modern State. What is far more important to-day in defining a regrouping of these territories into effective administrative units and effective units of democratic government is not merely the past history of their extent and associations, but the existing natural economic and social associations, coupled with an approximate similarity in their populations. Even the older and larger units, with the possible exception of Bavaria, do not form entities in this sense.

At this point we should like to emphasize certain broad divisions in the geographical structure of Germany which, omitting details, may perhaps be described as " Prussia versus the Rest "—a duality in the whole structure of German civilization which also finds broad geographical expression. This duality is based on the contrast in historical development between the Latinized lands of western and south-western Germany, and the " pagan " Germanic lands of north-eastern Germany. West and south in the Rhinelands were deeply impregnated by Roman and early Christian culture. Roman culture was absorbed by the German Franks, who had their chief centres of settlement in the Rhinelands and their chief capital in Frankfurt. These west German lands also became the lands of territorial disintegration in the Middle Ages and of independent small states. These, too, in the main, became Roman Catholic at the time of the Reformation, and, always, especially the southern States, offered stout resistance to the power of Prussia in the north and over the fate of the Reich after 1871 and again in 1919. On the other hand, the essentially German tradition, as many Germans would describe it, has its roots in the life and organization of the Saxon tribes in the lowlands east of the Elbe with their chief town centres on the northern edge of the Harz, the first capitals of the Saxon Emperors in the tenth and eleventh centuries, moving later eastwards to Brandenburg, and finally settling in Berlin. Here, the Saxons were the most recalcitrant of all the German tribes to be conquered and converted by the Franks. They retained and cherished much of their old pagan tradition, legal code, customs and so on. It was from this nucleus that the lands of Brandenburg and the Baltic shores and East Prussia were colonized. It was these territories that became the kingdom of Prussia with its historic nucleus in Brandenburg on the Elbe as an outgrowth from Lower Saxony (*Niedersachsen*). These lands were for the most part large undivided territories, under the direct control of their kings, where feudalism on the large estates died hard, as opposed to the small peasant holdings in the west—both the productive vine areas in the Rhinelands and the poorer farm lands in the uplands. These northern lands were gradually incorporated into Prussia, which also managed to push westwards into the Romanized lands on the lower Rhine. The Prussian spirit of totalitarianism and autocratic control stands in marked contrast to the more democratic spirit of the west and the south-west, especially in the Rhinelands. And it is this spirit which is now not simply inherent in Nazism, but blatantly announced as its basis—the revival of the Wagnerian cult of the early Saxon, the revival of pagan customs, and of tribal, so-called " folk " traits with roots in so-called " tribal differences ". All this is a direct attack on Western Christianity and it is difficult to see how the traditionally independent and self-governing States of the south can sincerely blend their ideals and aspirations with such a cult. German civilization, therefore, is a double thing with many geographical variations, and in large measure it can be traced to the contrast between the Romanized Franks, who settled in the Rhineland after the German folk migrations, and the Saxon civilization of the north-eastern lowlands, which spread in the Middle Ages eastwards, was crystallized in the amalgam of Prussianism under the Hohenzollerns, and finds its culminating expression in the Nazi doctrines and its paganistic cults. This broad contrast is emphasized, not complicated, by the usual distinction that is drawn between north Germany and south Germany, with their differences in dialect, tradition and the like, and the emergence of the Prussian State covering all the Northern Lowland. For the whole of the south was deeply affected by Roman Christianity, in spite of the fact that Munich was the birthplace of Nazism. The problem for the Germans is to permit the free development of the democratic spirit, if such we may call it, in the south and west, and to crush the unity of Prussia, and bring its component Provinces to the same level of government and democratic consciousness as the southern States. At any rate, this is the logical alternative to the trend of centralization in Berlin, which has been emphasized under the Nazis.

II

What then shall be the basis of a new set of political units as component elements in the new Reich? The proposals of the various bodies adopted, in general, the exisiting political pattern, with the absorption into it of all the small territories. This, as we have just indicated, is not enough. Others have sought a basis in the tribal areas of the old *Volksstämme* which show the regional differences in dialect, tradition, temperament and folk-lore. Special investigations of particular areas are based on various criteria, sometimes with the deliberate aim of supporting a contention for territorial gain. Many schemes for such a division of the Reich have been made. The most effective units are to be found (subject, however, to a clearly defined policy as to area and population), not in historical units, nor in existing divisions, nor in cultural associations, but in the natural entities of modern activity, interests and organization that are inherent in the structure of society. These afford the widest basis of assessment for measuring that homogeneity which is the essential basis for an effective political unit. Professor Hugo Preuss prepared a constitution in November 1918 for the new Weimar Republic. This was to be a federal State with Free States or *Länder* of roughly equal. size, with at least a million inhabitants. He envisaged sixteen States (Fig. 3)—Prussia (East and West), Silesia, Brandenburg, Lower Saxony, Upper Saxony, Hesse, Thuringia, Westphalia, Rhineland, Baden, Wurtemberg, Bavaria, Austria, Berlin, Vienna, and the Hansa cities of Hamburg, Bremen and Lübeck. Preuss' scheme failed owing to the opposition of the existing State governments, notably that of Prussia, and of the National Assembly in

1919. The question of a *Neugliederung* raised so many difficulties that the National Assembly shelved it. The root difficulty seems to have been that it was held, on the one hand, that the new central Reich government should displace the Prussian government, and the Prussian provinces should rank as the other *Länder* ; while, on the other hand, it was argued that in view of the international situation, the strength and unity of the

FIG. 3.—New Political Divisions proposed by H. Preuss (1918).
(After Vogel.)

Prussian government should be maintained at any price. The last view won, and Preuss' scheme for the new territorial organization of the Reich failed in its immediate purpose. The National Assembly, however, recommended the establishment of a Central Committee for the New Territorial Organization of the Reich (*Zentralstelle für Gliederung des Reiches*) in 1920, but this body produced no tangible results and was abolished in 1929. The only important change it effected was the creation of Thuringia as a unified *Land* out of many small fragments by a *Reichsgesetz* in 1920.

Other schemes have been put forward to remedy the defects of the constitution and the territorial organization. A conference of leading ministers from each *Land* was called by the Reich government in 1928 to discuss the problem. It declared that a new territorial organization was necessary, that the dualism of

FIG. 4.—New Political Divisions proposed by Dr. Luther.
(After Vogel.)

Reich and *Land* should be abolished, and that twenty-one *Länder* roughly of equal area and population, should be established with the provinces of Prussia standing as equals with the old States. Another scheme was elaborated for the *Bund zur Erneuerung des Reiches*, founded in 1928, by the Reichschancellor, Dr. Luther (Fig. 4). This scheme differed fundamentally from that of Preuss in that Prussia was to remain as a single political unit (*Reichsland*), directly controlled by the Reich government. This new *Reichsland* was to consist of twelve existing provinces of Prussia (with Berlin as a separate province), together with Thuringia, Hesse, Mecklenburg (Schwerin and Strelitz) and the two Hansa cities of Hamburg and Bremen. Other small *Länder* were to be absorbed into the neighbouring Prussian provinces to form five new divisions. In addition, there were to be four provinces outside the *Reichsland*, with a greater measure of administrative independence— Saxony, Bavaria, Baden and Wurtemberg.

The schemes of Preuss and Luther both adhere closely to the existing divisions, grouping some of them and abolishing all the outliers. They have the great advantage of adhering to the existing framework rather than elaborating an entirely new system with entirely new boundaries as some radical schemes suggest. Nevertheless, such schemes cannot give adequate recognition in detail to the facts of the distribution of population and social and economic associations, such as is essential for the creation of effective political units.

Walther Vogel [1] suggested in 1932, in summing up the spate of literature and discussion on the subject, that the existing political units be adhered to as closely as possible ; that local studies be undertaken to examine the distribution of settlement, traffic movements, economic and social relations, and the historical development of the existing political divisions, in order to facilitate the definition of new provinces and the clear delineation of their boundaries. The new province, he also stipulated, should conform to a standard population rather than a standard area, and this not only so that the province should be adequately represented in the *Reichsrat*, but so that it would be able to lead a balanced economic and cultural life, that is, it should be able to support a University, technical schools, museums, libraries, theatres, concerts, etc., and, we would add, the complete apparatus of representative government. He also lends support to the view that Berlin, Hamburg and Bremen should be independent provinces.

During the last twenty years the central Reich government has established its own nation-wide organization for many *ad hoc* purposes independent of the *Länder*—partly because the latter vary so much in size, partly to short-circuit the governments of the *Länder* which might grow too powerful. This applies to

---

[1] Walther Vogel, professor of historical geography in the University of Berlin, has made a special study of this problem in all its aspects in *Reichsgliederung und Reichsreform in Vergangenheit und Gegenwart* (*1932*). He was a friend of Preuss and took an important part in the proposals for the framing of the new politico-geographical pattern in 1919.

finance, administration, social administration (unemployment insurance, etc.), control of waterways, education and so on. The following are some examples given by Vogel.[1]

	Number of Divisions.
Prussian Provinces and *Länder* outside Prussia	30
Prussian *Regierungsbezirke*	35
Bavarian *Regierungsbezirke*	8
Other *Länder*	14
Landesfinanzämter	26
Landesarbeitsämter	13
Hauptversorgungsämter	14
Reichsbahndirektion	30
Oberpostdirektion	45

This process, known as *Aushöhlung*, by establishing an independent regional system of Reich government, parallel to and independent of that of the *Länder*, has undermined and weakened the authority of the latter, and has been the cause of a great deal of friction. It has also resulted in greater concentration of authority in Berlin. In the realm of taxation, " *Reich* and *Land* are like a married couple, when the husband earns the money, the wife pays it out, but they do not tell each other what the income is and what the money is spent for." [2]

The Reich is divided into provinces for a great variety of purposes—by departments of the Reich government as noted above, by industrial concerns for the transaction of business or the distribution of supplies from central offices, and by trade and professional organizations. Although these provinces differ considerably and are naturally based on the existing political divisions, they often reflect a necessary regard for such considerations as community of economic interest and activities. One of the most significant groups is the *Wirtschaftskammer*, the regional chambers of commerce that are subordinate to the *Reichswirtschaftskammer*. Each provincial chamber has on it representatives of local industrial and trade interests for each *Bezirk* in the province, and it also cares for the interests of all employed persons. There are seventeen of these regional groupings : East Prussia, Silesia, Brandenburg, Pomerania, Nordmark, Bremen, Lower Saxony (*Niedersachsen*), Düsseldorf (*Regierungsbezirk*), Westphalia and Lippe, Rhineland, Hesse, Central Germany (*Mitteldeutschland*), Saxony (*Sachsen*), Bavaria, Karlsruhe, Wurtemberg and *Regierungsbezirk* Sigmaringen, and the Saar-Palatinate (*Saarpfalz*). In addition, there are

[1] W. Vogel, *Deutsche Reichsgliederung und Reichsreform in Vergangenheit und Gegenwart*, 1932, p. 96.
[2] Vogel, op. cit., p. 97.

the *Industrie-* and *Handelskammern* which cover smaller districts and embrace all employed persons ; they also have legal authorities and care for the interests of industry and trade in their districts, functioning directly under the control of the *Reichswirtschaftskammer*. These small districts give a particularly clear indication of local economic relations, and to their wider economic relations in the major provinces with which they are associated. There are nearly a hundred of these districts. A related body is the Ministry of Labour (*Reichsarbeitsministerium*), which handles labour questions, such as unemployment, insurance, etc., in each of its districts (*Landesarbeitsämter*). These districts of the *Reichsarbeitsministerium* are thirteen in number with 359 smaller *Arbeitsämter*. They are as follows : East Prussia, Silesia, Brandenburg, Pomerania, Nordmark (Schleswig-Holstein, Hamburg, Lübeck, Mecklenburg, part of Oldenburg, and the districts of Niedersachsen lying on the south bank of the Elbe opposite Hamburg), *Niedersachsen* (most of Hanover, Brunswick, Bremen, Oldenburg, Schaumburg-Lippe), Westphalia, Rhineland, Hesse, Central Germany (*Mitteldeutschland*) (broadly Province Saxony, *Land* Thuringia and *Land* Anhalt), Saxony, Bavaria, South-west Germany. The organization established by the Nazi government for the settlement of labour disputes—the *Treuhänder der Arbeit*—also has a Reich-wide division into the following districts—East Prussia, Silesia, Brandenburg, Pomerania, Nordmark, Lower Saxony (*Niedersachsen*), Westphalia, Rhineland, Hesse, Central Germany (*Mitteldeutschland*), Saxony, Bavaria, South-west Germany, and Saar-Palatinate. These are important examples of the many divisions of the Reich adopted for purposes of Reich administration and for the care of economic interests.

Another important sphere of regional organization is connected with regional planning (*Landesplanung*), although such organizations differ in origin from the above in that they are groupings of local government authorities formed, as in Britain, voluntarily for the purpose of fact-finding and making recommendations for joint problems of physical planning—or, more correctly, inter-town planning. As in other countries, these were in the first place voluntary, with, however, one very important exception. Such organizations came into being entirely since the last war, although Dr. Robert Schmidt just before the last war put forward the case for the formation of a single planning authority for the Ruhr industrial area. Such a body, known as the *Ruhrkohlenbezirk Siedlungsverband,* was established in 1920, with Dr. Schmidt as its first President, with full legal powers for dealing with traffic, housing, open spaces and railway traffic for the region as a whole.   The region extends as a belt from near Hamm in the east, across the Rhine westwards to the Belgian frontier, and has a population of about 4½ million inhabitants on 5,000 square kilometres.   Voluntary regional planning organizations, without any legal authority to carry their proposals into effect, were established afterwards in the Reich, and these usually have their centres in the great cities.   Thus, to quote a few examples, a Greater Hamburg regional planning authority was formed in the 'twenties, covering the area within 30 kilometres of the city centre, and similar bodies were established around the other great cities, such as Frankfurt and Cologne.   Many of these authorities took as their geographical limits the boundaries of the political divisions, usually the *Regierungsbezirk.*   Of special interest are the ,elaborate investigations and recommendations made by the *Mitteldeutschland* regional planning body for the future development of the recently and rapidly developed brown-coalfield in the middle Elbe basin, an entirely new industrial area that overlaps the boundaries of Prussia, Saxony, Thuringia, Anhalt and many small territorial outliers.   Its report and problems will be discussed later.   All this development, as in Britain, is piecemeal and voluntary and without central co-ordination, and the Nazis have organized the whole of the Reich into regions, incorporating these planning authorities, for purposes of physical and economic and social planning.

It will also be obvious that for statistical purposes, the State or *Land* and the Prussian Province, with their interlocking territories, are inadequate for the appraisal of conditions in compact geographical areas.   For this reason, for example, the German census uses, in addition to the existing political divisions, a set of economic units (*Wirtschaftsgebiete*), grouping together all the separate political territories in each unit.   These are as follows : East Prussia, Pomerania, Berlin-Brandenburg, Silesia, Saxony, Mitteldeutschland (Province Saxony, Anhalt, Thuringia), Bavaria together with the Palatinate, North Elbe (Hamburg and Schleswig-Holstein), Niedersachsen (including roughly the province Hanover, and the *Länder* of Brunswick, Oldenburg, Bremen and Lippe), Rhineland-Westphalia, Hesse (Hesse-Nassau and the province of Hesse), and the South-west.

From this brief enumeration of regional divisions used for a variety of purposes one notices at once the recurrence of names and groupings that have no political existence. This is the kind of geographical grouping that is inherent in the organization of modern society, and is, in fact, based upon the actual areas of modern regional associations. In east Germany, the *ad hoc* units consistently conform to the Prussian provinces. Elsewhere, we may note in particular several groupings that do not appear on the political map. Central Germany or *Mitteldeutschland*, it will be noted, is the name usually given to the whole or parts of the *Länder* of Anhalt, Thuringia and Province Saxony—the new brown-coal industrial area. Lower Saxony or *Niedersachsen* has its nucleus in the Province of Hanover and includes many small political divisions in and around it. The south-west includes usually the *Länder* of Wurtemberg and Baden. Rhine-Main or *Rhein-Main* includes the area around Frankfurt, comprising Hesse and Hesse-Nassau, with variations in limits.

We have already said that a vast amount of work has been done by both public and private authorities in Germany on the geographical structure of the regions of Germany. Public bodies have financed such investigations. There are numerous bodies attached to the Universities that have encouraged research on all aspects of regional problems. There are comprehensive atlases for several of the regions that are models of their kind and might serve as examples for the preliminary work in regional reconstruction that is needed in this country as a basis for future planning in all its aspects. Thus, there are atlases of Lower Saxony (*Niedersachsen*), Silesia, Pomerania, Westphalia, Alsace-Lorraine, Saar, Rhenish Palatinate, and Rhine-Main. There are several exhaustive and authoritative atlases for the Reich as a whole showing economic data— agriculture, industry and commerce—in which respects we in this country have only just made a start. Studies of regional, physical, economic and commercial problems are numerous in the publications of scientific societies. Another aspect of this work is the proposals actually put forward by individuals, based on various criteria, for the regional division of the Reich that is, in their view, best suited to serve the needs of a new regional reconstruction of the Reich. Post-war political reformers, as we have seen, aimed at the creation of regions that should be effective political and cultural units, but should also, in the interests of expediency, fit as closely as possible with existing political units. These schemes in varying measure fail to give adequate weight

to the facts of regional economic activity and orientation.   However, in the last twenty years a good deal of work on these lines
has been done.   Thus, Erwin Scheu, professor of geography at
Königsberg, has thoroughly examined the *innere Verflechtung* of
the Reich (Fig. 8).   He recognizes twenty-two smaller regions
(*Wirtschaftsbezirke*) and nine larger provinces (*Wirtschaftsprovinzen*)
basing his study mainly on the facts of industrial and agricultural
production and commerce.   The larger provinces are the Baltic

FIG. 5.—New Political Divisions proposed by A. Weitzel (*Frankfurter
Entwurf*) (1928) on basis of spheres of influence of chief cities.
(After Vogel.)

province (Schleswig-Holstein, Mecklenburg, Pomerania, East
Prussia), Niedersachsen, Berlin-Brandenburg, Silesia, Central
Germany, Rhenish-Westphalia, Rhine-Main, South-west and
Bavaria.   Weitzel, a public administrator of Frankfurt, made an
investigation of the Rhine-Main region in 1928 and, using this
as a basis, suggested a division of the Reich into twelve regions
(Fig. 5) as determined by " the economic interests of the separate
sections of the Reich, their geographical contiguity, their social
structure, and cultural unity ".   Many other schemes have been
prepared—some taking account primarily of the historic units,
others of cultural data (Fig. 7), others of the sources and distri-

bution of power as the basis of economic activity and orientation (Fig. 6), and. still others on other assessments in an attempt to fit a particular point of view or to suit particular desiderata.[1]

The Nazis placed in the forefront of their programme in 1933 a co-ordinated plan of regional and national development. On March 29, 1935, a National Board (*Reichsstelle*) was created to regulate the land requirements of public bodies " in a way that suits the needs of people and state ".   On June 26, 1935,

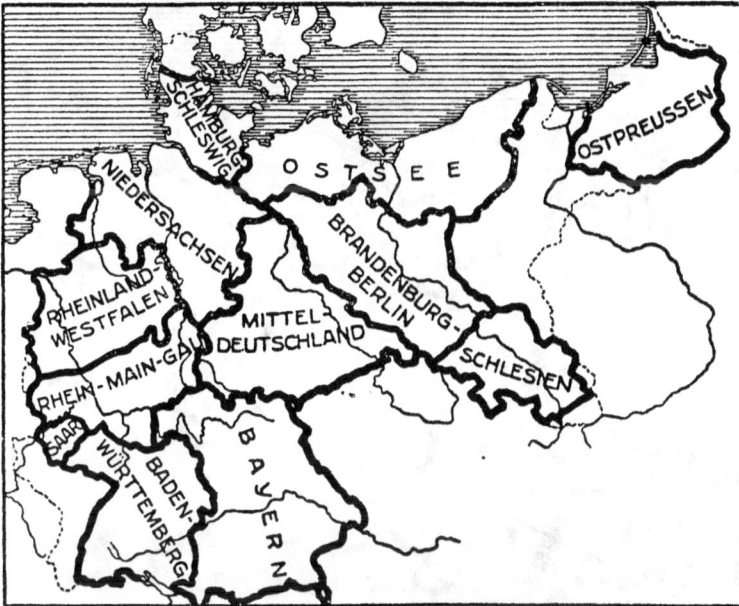

FIG. 6.—New Political Divisions proposed by Baumann on basis of services of power and railway traffic.
(After Vogel.)

the title of National Planning Board (*Reichsstelle für Raumordnung*) was conferred on this body, and to it was entrusted the " comprehensive co-ordinated planning of the whole Reich ".   To facilitate this, the *Reichsstelle* was made responsible for the organization and control of all national and regional planning authorities.

A framework was established by the National Planning Board

[1] It should be noted that such proposals appeared in great numbers in the 'twenties, when the whole problem, as raised by the first Weimar Assembly, was right to the fore. The Nazis have discouraged the private publication of such proposals, but research has gone on and solutions have been effected from the centre, dealing summarily with questions of heated controversy.

in February 1936 (Fig. 9). The Reich was divided into twenty-three planning regions (*Planungsräume*) which generally coincide with the provinces of Prussia and the *Länder*. The Ruhr region (*Ruhrsiedlungsbezirk*), Berlin, and Hamburg remain as separate regions. In each region the chief planning authority was the supreme representative of the Reich (*Reichstatthalter*, or, in the provinces, *Oberpräsident*), who was directly responsible to the

Fig. 7.—New Political Divisions proposed by W. Tuckermann on basis of cultural criteria (*naturgemässe Stammeszusammenhänge*). (After Vogel.)

National Board. The main organization was the Regional Planning Federation (*Landesplanungsgemeinschaft*), a body with statutory and executive powers, on which were represented all facets of activity in the region—social, economic, political, administrative and academic. This body was to be responsible for examining the conditions and needs of its region and for constructing a comprehensive regional plan. The actual work of planning lay in the hands of the Regional Planner. The Board also established a central body for the direction and co-ordination of planning research (*Reichsarbeitsgemeinschaft für Raumforschung*).

FIG. 8.—Economic Provinces.
(After Scheu.)

Twenty-two economic regions, including Berlin. The boundaries follow the limits of the smaller administrative units (*Kreise* and *Oberämter*). These twenty-two regions are grouped by Scheu into nine major economic provinces (from *Erde und Wirtschaft*, Heft 1, 1927).

Subordinate to this body groups were formed in most Universities to co-ordinate the investigation of general conditions and specific problems of their regions.

The purpose of these regional planning regions may be gleaned from one of the many public speeches made at their inception by Reichsminister Kerrl, head of the *Reichsstelle für Raumordnung*, on January 21, 1936.

Fundamentally it is our endeavour to direct all changes in the German State, whether effected by settlement, commercial

FIG. 9.—Nazi Regional Planning Districts (1936).
(From *American Geographical Review*, 1938.)

developments, or the erection of industrial establishments or through other demands on the land, on a basis of planning and foresight, in the common interests of the people and State ; and also to place all such developments under the guidance and security of the State. In this connection, three great problems may be emphasized : a thorough clearance of the urban agglomerations in the industrial areas and great cities, a legacy from the unregulated, planless growth of the past ; the planned penetration and economic development of those regions that hitherto have been relatively neglected and unprotected, and particularly those in the east ; and finally, the working out of comprehensive plans, such as organically must emerge if the guiding tenets and principles of planning by the State are to find logical application for the common good of people and State.

The *Reichsstelle* in Berlin demanded just before the outbreak of war a general planning report from each of the twenty-three planning regions (*Allgemeine Raumordnungsskizzen*). According to an article published in 1939, these plans were to serve a double purpose. First, the regional *Planungsgemeinschaften* will have a general survey of the existing conditions, which will serve as a basis for future detailed research and proposals ; second, the central *Reichsstelle* will have a composite view of the conditions in the various regions and the priority of their needs. While freedom of exposition was left to the regional authorities, the following topics were briefed for special emphasis—housing shortage ; uncertainty, scope, and duration of employment in industry and building ; deficiencies in agriculture owing to the lack of technical resources ; soil fertility ; and any increase of rural emigration, or of growth of cities and industrial areas. Special attention was to be given to frontier districts. This programme aimed at the security of the food supply, the revival of depressed areas (*Notstandsgebiete*), and the " strengthening " (*Sicherung*) of frontier districts. Its political and strategic motives are obvious.

It is of the utmost importance to realize that the appropriate scientific authorities have been marshalled by the Nazis for the systematic study of geographical relationships (*Raumforschung*) with a view to planning—in the short run, the programme was undoubtedly designed to serve strategic as well as social needs. *Raum-* or *Landforschung* and *Raum-* or *Landesplanung* have been catchwords in Germany since 1933 and have attracted the energies of scientists and have reached the wider public as an urgent social problem. But this is not a Nazi innovation ; they have canalized and organized through centralization trends that had been evident since 1919. They have established a framework for the co-ordinated physical and social planning of the Reich, which will undoubtedly figure large in the regional reconstruction of Germany at the peace, although in a spirit very different, we must assume, from that of the Nazis.

A second unit of regional organization established by the Nazis before the war affords the basis for the elaborate structure of Party organization (Fig. 10). This unit is the *Gau*, which is the highest, in size and authority, of a descending series of five areas. The main considerations in forming these districts or *Gaue* were evidently equal population, a large measure of group feeling, and ease of accessibility to a central administrative headquarters. They adhere closely to political divisions by groupings, but frequently cut across them. Some changes have been made in these areas during the war, notably in the expansion of the Silesian area to include all Upper Silesia to

FIG. 10.—Nazi Party Districts (*Gaue*) (pre-War).
(From *American Geographical Review*, 1938.)

the pre-1918 frontiers, and the realignment of *Gaue* in the west with the absorption of Alsace-Lorraine and Luxemburg into the Reich.

These two units, the Planning Region and the Party Region, are clearly of fundamental importance in the life of the Nazi Reich. The planning regions are as follows (spelled in German) —Rheinland, Saarpfalz, Westfalen, Hannover, Rhein-Main, Kurhessen, Baden, Württemberg, Thüringen, Bayern, Sachsen, Anhalt, Schleswig-Holstein, Mecklenburg-Lübeck, Brandenburg, Pommern, Ostpreussen, Sachsen, Schlesien, Oldenburg-Bremen,

and the Ruhrgebiet, Berlin and Hamburg, the last including the
whole of the agglomeration of Greater Hamburg. The Party
Gaue are generally similar to the Planning Regions except in the
populous areas in western Germany where they are smaller.
Thus, Rheinland falls into the *Gaue* of Essen-Düsseldorf, Köln-
Aachen, and Koblenz-Trier. In the north-west there are
Weser-Ems, Nord-Westfalen, Süd-Westfalen, Ost-Hannover, Süd-
Hannover. The planning region of Sachsen-Anhalt forms two
Gaue, Magdeburg-Anhalt and Halle-Merseburg. Bavaria, one
planning region, falls into five *Gaue*, Main-Franken, Franken,
Bäyrische-Ostmark, Schwaben, and München-Oberbayern. In
eastern and south-eastern Germany planning regions and *Gaue*
are coincident with the political provinces.

Thus, to sum up. After 1871 the new Reich was a loose
federation of States, each of which had a large measure of real
self-government, though the federation was completely dominated
by Prussia. After the last war, in spite of the strong movements
for decentralization from Berlin and a large measure of autonomy
free from the control of Berlin, the pendulum swung in the opposite direction. Thus, the Weimar National Assembly decreed
virtually complete control of taxation by the Reich government,
a most momentous decision, and established a Defence Ministry,
and centralized all the State railway concerns as a single State
organization (*Reichsbahngesellschaft*). The States or *Länder* as they
were called in the Weimar Republic, remained responsible for
justice, education, police and social welfare, but controlled
virtually no taxation. In effect, the whole system of taxation was
controlled by the Reich and the *Länder* received their finances
from the pocket of the central Treasury.

This centralization has become even more marked under the
Nazi regime, for an avowed and much vaunted aim of Nazi
domestic policy has been to co-ordinate systems of law and government throughout the Reich, and to regroup the political divisions
of the Reich within the new framework, though depriving them
of every semblance of real self-government by reducing the status
of the *Länder* to that of mere units of administration with a greatly
swollen bureaucratic machine.

III. The Concept of the Region

The problem of regional reconstruction is by no means
peculiar to Germany. It is common to all the countries of

Western civilization, that have experienced a revolution in their structure in the last 100 years which has made their centuries-old political divisions, and, in large measure, the machinery of local government, hopelessly antiquated, and the patching-up methods adopted so far in adapting them to the new space-relations are inefficient and the system of administrative units and the functions of such units need drastic overhauling. The whole trend of interest in these problems may be summed up under the two heads of Regionalism and Regional Reconstruction. These problems are not peculiar to Germany, for they have found much attention in this country during the war under the new sense of urgency, although it must be admitted that they received very little public attention in the inter-war period. In Britain, the main question is one of building up units of democratic representative government rather than units of administration. In Germany, on the other hand, it is a question of creating a federation of Provinces, *Länder*, or whatever they may be called, that will also permit some form of democratic government and co-operation, in place of the centuries-old tradition of sovereign independence, which in its traditional trappings must go, with an up-to-date system erected in its place.

There are three distinct aspects of this general problem of creating new political units. First, there is the set of existing political divisions, which with all their shortcomings have existed for a long time and are, in fact, the basis of the present system of government, organization and many associations. Such divisions are by no means sacrosanct. The whole problem we are discussing is to create new provinces which shall be more in accord with modern groupings. But the existing boundaries should be used as far as possible, rather than be replaced by entirely new ones. Second, there are regions in Germany whose peoples have a feeling of community, based upon such facts as dialect, customs, temperament and history. It is customary in Germany to regard the social groupings as identical with the ancient *Volksstämme*. They are rather the product of association and common experience through many centuries. Frequently these groupings have grown from within, and are identical with a single state or province. But they also frequently cut across these divisions to form units which have no political existence, but are very real in the public mind. Third, there are the modern regions of social and economic associations that are inherent in the structure of society, their unity being due primarily to integration around the great cities, emphasized by the unity 'of practical organization in their economic activities. It is upon this third set of considerations above all else that a new pattern of units should be based.

We consider a region to be a geographical unit of economic and social activity and organization. We have defined it as an area of inter-related activities and kindred interest and organization. It is an entity of human space relationships, which are effected through the medium of the route pattern and the urban centres. Such a region, therefore, embraces the complex and closely woven fabric of intercourse by which are effected the transfer of goods, and the distribution of services, news, and ideas, the very bases of society. This conception does not involve the idea of a water-tight compartment, nor does such integration mean that linear boundaries can be defined in reality. It does maintain that such a region has a core and that it is normally centred upon the principal cities. Such a region is a unit in the sense that its people are bound together economically and socially far more than with adjacent areas. This unity is due to three sets of conditions : first, the predominance of a group of activities—agriculture, industry, commerce and service—that are the same or complementary and interdependent through the interchange of goods and services ; second, the dominance of both movements and activities by one or more great cities, that are at once the chief centres of affairs and the chief centres of radial routes and traffic ; third, the common bonds of historical development—political development, cultural associations and tradition—both in the economic and cultural senses, in spite of the fact that these associations often cut across old-established political boundaries.

The unity of such a region is due, however, not merely to the radial movements of persons and goods to and from the great city centres. It is due also to the exchange of goods between its parts and, in consequence, to the common interests between them. It follows that in rural areas there will be no such clearly defined geographical orientation of commerce as in a densely populated industrial area. A densely populated industrial area shows a clearly defined pattern of settlement and a close and complicated network of routes, which, in the form of population and traffic density maps, may serve as main bases of regional characterization. Such a region should not, we repeat,

be envisaged as an area with clearly defined limits.   It has a core
and wide indeterminate zones between it and the neighbouring
regions.   It is in the nature of things that the heart of a region
should be its nuclear cities and that towards the periphery relations should be more complex and areas transitional.   The
transitional areas often are centred around a town which has
relations with two or more big metropolitan cities or regions.
Boundaries, however, may be defined in detail, after the main
nucleus of the region is determined, by following some vital rela-
tionship—and this, of course, will vary from place to place—
such as local community feeling, a change in the character of industry or the distribution of population, or a marked break in
local associations as between one town and another.   Moreover,
political boundaries of long standing are, for that very reason,
often real cultural and economic divides, and it is in any case
most practicable to follow wherever possible the boundaries of
districts of the order of the German *Kreise*.

From the point of view of assessing these regional associations
we may pursue each aspect a step further.

The distribution of agriculture and industry by small statistical
units gives a basis for the location, extent and main activities of
what may be called the *static* or fixed activities—in the sense that
each is tied down to a particular place, be it a farm or a factory,
as opposed to the *dynamic* or mobile activities, that is, the activities
concerned with moving goods and people from place to place
along the road and the railway and the waterway.   The factory,
or the farm, or the residence, can, if accurately mapped, give
no clue as to integration although this is necessary as a basis to
its investigation.   Thus, the idea of an industrial region is an
area that in all its parts has a dominant group of inter-related
industries.   The movement of persons, from the point of view of
regional integration, is concerned with the movement from home
to work-place, be it factory or office, and this may range up to
a distance of a one-hour journey—time and cost being the
determining factors.   The movement of goods is concerned with
the movement of specialized production goods from factory to
factory, port to factory, etc., and with the collection and distribution of goods from producer to producer or factory to factory
and from producer to consumer.   In the latter sense, in particular,
the whole apparatus of transport, commerce, and finance, is
concentrated in towns.   The movement of ideas and services is
in a different category and can best be assessed by the area

covered by services and organizations, and here one has to consider the boundaries of the State and its divisions, both in the
past and in the present, as frames for the organization of these
functions and as deterrents to their efficient execution.

The distribution of towns shows a fairly regular spacing
according to their size. Every town is essentially and basically
a centre of commerce, administration and culture (in the broadest
sense) for a surrounding, vaguely defined territory. The smallest
centre of this kind is the market town. Towns of different
grades offering an ever-greater variety of services are more widely
spaced in such a way that a town of lower order tends to develop
equidistant from the two of higher order. In this way we may
envisage an ideal pattern of distribution in which every town,
and especially the bigger cities with which we are primarily
concerned, tends to have a series of six towns of next lower order
on the borders of its zone of service and influence, and the
latter in virtue of their relative remoteness have a high measure
of independent status for their territories, free from outside competition. This has been true of the past ; it is true to-day.
It is a fundamental law of the distribution of towns as service
centres.

While it is true that every town has a service area, the nature
and potency of its influence varies normally with increasing
distance from it and is extremely vague and indeterminate in
a wide outer zone, where its relations merge with those of other
local towns and more distant towns of the same rank as itself.
Only one kind of territory provides us with a framework which
is clearly defined with a rigid frame for aspects of administration
and economic life—namely, the political unit. Throughout the
history of Germany, as in other countries, the pattern of political
divisions reveals a changing kaleidoscope of small units, forming
on the map a crazy-coloured quilt. But closer scrutiny will
reveal that many of these divisions in their central areas, and
frequently their frontiers, are permanent. Often, too, one can
trace in their historical and cultural development the close
association of geographically contiguous sectors of the mosaic.
Such areas through centuries of history have been closely
associated in their political, cultural and economic development.
Many of these historical features are still a part of popular feeling and usage and these must count as real factors of modern
regional associations in addition to those that are more narrowly
defined as economic. Scattered territories have far more in

common with the States in which they are embedded than with their parent States from which they are often geographically remote. Such is the case, for example, with the Prussian district of Hohenzollern that lies in Wurtemberg. Clusters of contiguous political territories, as, for instance, in the Rhinelands around Frankfurt, though administratively separate, have common traits of culture and history. The politico-cultural province is almost always traceable by a permanent political core, such as the old kingdom of Hanover and its predecessors. Very often there occur on its borders smaller territories that, like the towns noted above, may be closely interrelated and are largely independent units, but have close relations with the two or more contiguous major provinces. Indeed, the political pattern sometimes reveals a veritable " shatter belt " between two politico-cultural units. This is pre-eminently illustrated by the territories of the middle and lower Weser lands between the lower Rhinelands and *Niedersachsen* or Lower Saxony.

After a thorough investigation on the above lines we have prepared a map of the economic regions of Germany together with their chief city centres (Fig. 11). This book is a more detailed elaboration of the structure and essential unifying characteristics of each of these regions. A word is needed on the method of compilation of the regional divisions, as shown on this map. It is greatly reduced and generalized and involved careful study of the regional associations throughout the Reich and the definition of each region as to its characteristics and limits. This is the subject of each of the regional descriptions in the following pages. Each region was determined by considering the various nation-wide regional divisions, the proposals for new political divisions, the existing distribution of industry, agriculture, and, above all, the commercial relationships between adjacent areas as defined by the movement of goods and persons, and general regional organization. The boundaries were drawn so as to follow the existing political divisions wherever possible, but they are smoothed out on this diagram, since our object is not to define new political divisions, nor to mark hard-and-fast lines, but to emphasize the location and character of the nuclear areas. Boundaries on this basis are often indeterminate. Further, the city centres are classified according to their importance as centres of regional integration. This may be estimated from the importance of their " regional " or, as they are called here, their " centralized " urban services. These are taken to include the total number of people, according to the census classification, engaged as officials (*Beamten*) and employees (*Angestellten*) in the following industries and handicrafts that are essentially regional in character : all engaged in the wholesale trades and publishing ; banking, insurance, etc. ; commerce ; and public and private service, excluding domestic service.[1]

It is the purpose of this book to give a brief pen-picture of

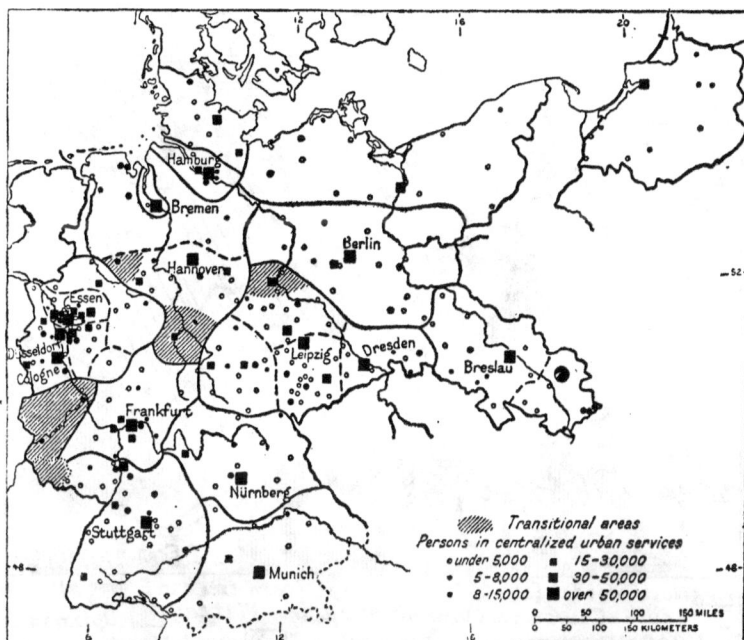

FIG. 11.—Economic Regions and their city centres as prepared by the present author.
(From *American Geographical Review*, 1938.)

each of the regions in Germany which have a large measure of unity in their history, and present activities and organization, and, consequently, in their interests and aspirations, regions which, by common agreement among German students, should, in principle, be adopted as Provinces in a new Reich. We are not concerned with the political or constitutional aspects of the problem, but with indicating the make-up of these regions and the basis of their unity. Moreover, quite apart from the question

[1] Otto Schlier, *Die Zentralen Orte des Deutschen Reichs, Zeitschrift der Gesellschaft für Erdkunde zu Berlin*, Nr. 5/6, 1937.

of territorial reorganization, this method of description provides
a sound geographical basis upon which to portray the lands and
peoples of Germany to the general reader.

The method of presentation of each region is the same,
though there are naturally differences of emphasis. The extent
of the region is determined primarily by the present and past
regional circulations as shown by the political divisions, cultural

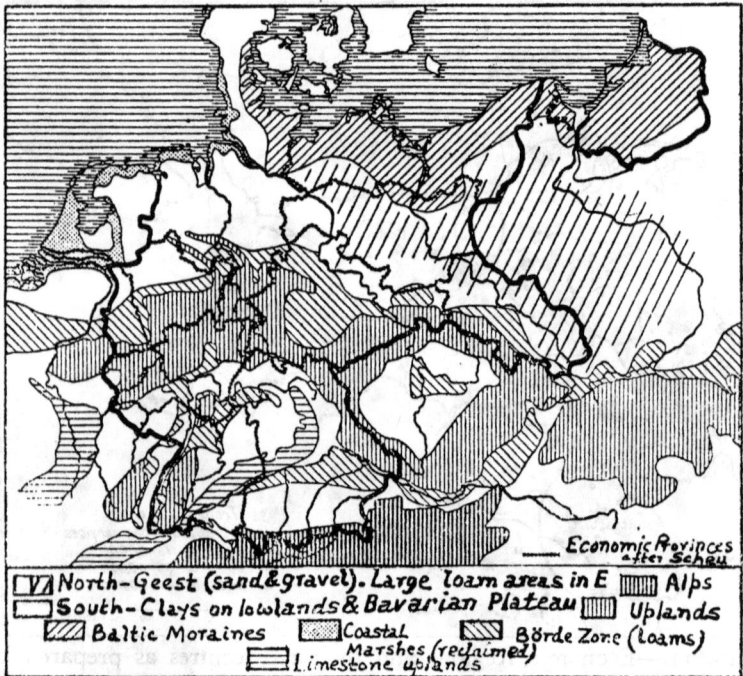

FIG. 11A.—Main Relief and Soil Regions.
(After Vogel.)

associations, economic activities and the dominance of the big
cities as outstanding foci of human movements and organization.
This assessment is basic to the presentation. But in each region
there are also stressed the elements of unity within it that make
up its sub-divisions. Thus, there are described the broad physical
background, emphasizing the character and importance of the
natural routeways and the chief seats of settlement ; the distribution and character of the chief types of farming and industry ;
the political divisions ; and traffic flows. Each major region is,
of course, characterized by considerable intrinsic diversity in

respect of each of these sets of conditions and these regional divisions are brought out. Finally since in all these respects the present can only be understood in terms of the past, the approach is throughout historical, and we have endeavoured to strike a balance between the economic, cultural, and political aspects of the problem of regional differentiation. The definition of specific boundaries, we repeat, is not a primary concern, but it should be pointed out that in studying each region, the existing boundaries of States, Provinces or their divisions are followed wherever practicable.

CHAPTER II

GERMANY AS A WHOLE

In this chapter we shall deal broadly with those aspects of
land and economy in Germany as a whole upon which regional
differentiations within it are based.   These are as follows : the
physical build of the land ; the politico-cultural units in the
State, formed through the geographical association of peoples in
history ; the present distribution of population as giving the fullest
indication of present regional differentiations ; and the modern
economic bases of these differentiations—agriculture, industry
and commerce.

I. The Land (Fig. 1)

Germany falls into two great physical divisions, the Northern
Lowland and the Central Uplands.   The Uplands are bordered
to the south by the great mountain system of the Alps, but only
the long narrow belt of lower mountains called the Prealps come
into Germany in southern Bavaria.   The drainage is to the
north, by the Rhine, Weser, Elbe and Oder.   The Danube in
the south is the only river flowing eastwards through south
Germany, leaving by the gorge between the Bohemian Forest
and the Alps before reaching the more open country near Vienna.
The Northern Lowland falls into two parts.   In the west, the
land is flat, almost at sea-level, with heath, moors, meadows, and
coastal marshes, and occasional patches of fertile, and in consequence, early settled land.   In the east, there is a great concentric arrangement of types of country, convex to the south and
parallel to the Baltic shore—a level and fertile coastal plain ;
wooded and lake-strewn hummocky uplands ; a zone, covering
the greater part of Brandenburg, of wide, flat, marshy, lake-strewn
valleys, and intervening, better drained, cultivated land ; and,
finally, a wide belt of heath-and-forest-covered uplands, forming
a great crescent from the Lüneburg Heath, south of and parallel
to the lower Elbe, the Fläming and Lusatian heaths, and their
continuation in northern Silesia and central Poland.
On the southern border of this northern plain and merging
into the Central Uplands is a zone, varying in width and occasionally interrupted by different types of country, of well-drained,

30

rolling country, with no forest or marsh, and forming a zone of prehistoric settlement and of human movements. It is the tillage zone *par excellence* of western and central Europe. This zone extends from northern France to southern Russia. In Germany it has three great embayments stretching southwards into the uplands, called the Cologne " Bay ", the Leipzig " Bay " and the Silesian " Bay ". It is known locally as the *Börde* and, for that reason, is sometimes called generally the *Börde* zone.

The Central Uplands consist of an alternation of wooded upland blocks and sheltered lowlands and plains. In general, the latter are below 2,000 ft. high, and the plateau blocks do not exceed 4,000 ft. at their highest. Thus, the lowlands and lower parts of the upland blocks are within the reach of cultivation— the upper limit of rye is about 2,000 ft. and the plateau blocks are usually thickly wooded, nowhere reaching the treeline though they often have extensive tracts of grass on their upper slopes. They offer no real barrier to movement or settlement.

The Central Uplands fall into three belts. In the north there are the wooded upland blocks of the rectangular Middle Rhine Plateau, and the uplands radiating from the Fichtelgebirge in the north-west corner of the Bohemian plateau. These include the Thuringian uplands and the Erzgebirge, while the Harz form an outlying isolated block to the north. Between these blocks are the Weser uplands drained by the river of that name and its tributaries and the Leine. These uplands form a wide zone of easy movement and fertile soils stretching, in patches, from northern Germany to the upper Rhine plain at Frankfurt. The lowland of Thuringia lies between the Harz and Thuringian uplands and from it lowland routes lead west to the Leine trough and the Weser at Göttingen and Kassel. The Rhine gorge itself from Bingen to Bonn offers the only easy passage from south to north across the Middle Rhine Plateau.

To the south of this belt are the smaller plateau blocks and more extensive and productive lowlands and plains of southern Germany. The lowlands include the fertile plain of the Rhine from Bingen upstream to Basel in Switzerland and of its right bank tributaries, the Main and the Neckar. The latter are enclosed by wooded rolling plateaus sloping gently outwards to the Danube in the south and to the basin in which Nürnberg is situated in the east, which is bounded to the east by the Bohemian Forest. The warm, dry climate of these sheltered lowlands makes them the most productive lands in Germany and the vine is their most important crop together with grain in the rolling plateaus of the middle basins of the Main and Neckar.

Finally, south of the Danube, there is the south Bavarian plateau. This has an average altitude of some 2,000 ft. rising gently to the foot of the Alps. It is roughly triangular-shaped, lying between the Danube and the Alps, narrowing westwards between the Alps and the Black Forest and eastwards between the Bohemian-Bavarian Forest and the Alps. Owing to its high altitude it has a relatively cool climate and has a cover of forest, marsh and lakes, with several fairly extensive patches of fertile land.

II. THE HISTORICAL PROVINCES (Fig. 12)

In the early Middle Ages with the end of Charles the Great's great empire, the Treaty of Verdun divided the Empire into three parts. Of these the central and eastern parts became the medieval German Reich. In the tenth century this fell into a number of great dukedoms, loose political units based in a large measure on common traits in the origins and history of their people, and well defined as to their central populous areas, and bordered by wide natural barriers of forest, mountain and marsh. Each of these dukedoms had as its nucleus the area of settlement of related tribal groups, settled in the forest-free, fertile areas, that had been occupied from prehistoric times. The main divisions of the dukedoms also corresponded with the areas of the bishoprics. The boundaries of these dukedoms, though at first vague and ill-defined, frequently became, with the closer settlement of the barrier zones between them, real and permanent cultural barriers, separating peoples with different dialects, culture forms and traditions, though all were members of the common Germanic stock. These dukedoms were Friesland on the northern coast lands ; Saxony, with two divisions, Eastphalia and Westphalia ; Franconia in the Main basin with two divisions, East and West ; Swabia in the south-west ; Bavaria from the Lech to the Enns and from the Alps to the Danube ; Upper and Lower Lorraine west of the Rhine to the Scheldt and the Argonne uplands beyond the river Meuse. A zone of border provinces (or *marks*)—like the marches in England against Scotland and Wales—were established against the Slavs beyond the Elbe and the Saale rivers on either side of the kingdom of Bohemia. East

of this belt lay the Slav dukedoms of Pomerania and Silesia that
were early incorporated into the Reich ; and Prussia, West and
East, beyond the lower Vistula, that became the main field of
conquest and colonization of the Teutonic Knights.

FIG. 12.—Historical Provinces.

Provinces based on the 1815 frontiers. The pre-1815 boundaries show the old
kingdom of Saxony and the city territories of Nürnberg and Bayreuth. The
bishoprics' temporal powers were abolished in 1815.

This medieval pattern in eastern Germany has remained
permanent to this day although the border provinces, while permanent in their cores, waxed and waned on their boundaries.
Two powers and states became dominant, Brandenburg, the
nucleus of Prussia, and Saxony in the middle Elbe basin, that
was finally whittled down in 1815 to the small state of Saxony.
In the west, on the other hand, in the early thirteenth century
there came about a confused pattern of " rags and tatters " of
land owing to the break up of all semblance of unity in the Reich
and the uncontrolled powers of feudal lords. The bishops had
the most extensive territories, many cities were independent,

C

and secular lords sought by warfare to increase and consolidate their territories. There was lacking any common system of Imperial law and order. Attempts were made by regional combinations of towns to protect their own interests, and in the sixteenth century and onwards the Emperors divided up the Reich into about a dozen areas or *Kreise* for the financing and recruiting of troops. The political map of 1790 revealed four great States, Prussia, Saxony, and, in the south, Bavaria and Wurtemberg. In addition, there were the extensive territories of the bishops and the Free Cities, that were found mainly in the south-west, together with the three city ports of Lübeck, Bremen, and Hamburg. This confusion of nearly four hundred sovereign units was reduced to about forty in 1815. At this time, too, the political divisions within the States were reorganized (as in France) in a hierarchy of units varying in name but all resembling the Prussian system, The latter included the Province, the *Regierungsbezirk* or Government district (cf. French *département*) and the *Kreis* or circle (cf. French *arrondissement*), with below it the *Amt*, which consisted of a group of several parishes (*gemeinde*) (cf. French *canton*). This set the pattern which, with a few changes, exists to-day. In 1871 there were twenty-five States. These included Prussia, the greatest of them all ; Anhalt, Brunswick, Lippe and Schaumburg-Lippe, all in the centre ; Mecklenburg-Schwerin and Mecklenburg-Strelitz ; the Free Cities of Lübeck, Bremen and Hamburg ; and, to the south of Prussia, Hesse, Baden, Wurtemburg, Bavaria and Saxony. There were in addition numerous small detached parts of these States in western Germany.

Through this changing political pattern one can trace the permanence of certain units and boundaries and recognize areas which through their permanence can be regarded as real cultural units with a feeling of kinship and unity based on tradition and temperament and a common culture heritage—house types, architecture, folk-lore, dress, and the like. These we have called politico-cultural provinces. In the west, these provinces show a close relation to the boundaries of the early tribal duchies. Bavaria has always retained the shape of its medieval dukedom, adding in 1815 the bishoprics of Würzburg and Bamberg in the valley of the Main in the north. From Franconia there emerged the bishoprics just noted, and, west of the Odenwald and Spessart uplands, at the northern end of the Rhine plain around Frankfurt, there appeared in 1815 five political units which together form one politico-cultural province that may be called, for convenience,

Hesse-Nassau. Beyond the Rhine appeared in 1815 the Rhenish Palatinate, an outlier of Bavaria. Swabia in the south-west split up into a bewildering pattern in the Middle Ages but has retained its cultural unity, though forming in 1815 the political divisions of Alsace, Baden, Wurtemberg and German Switzerland. Each of these units is of old standing and is separated from its neighbours by natural barriers of wooded uplands— the Franconian Jura, the Black Forest and the Vosges. In central Germany, Hesse had its nucleus in the lowland routes which ran from Frankfurt northwards; and Thuringia was centred on the lowland commanded by Erfurt. The latter lowland was united to form one geographical unit, the State of Thuringia, in 1920.

The middle Elbe basin above Magdeburg falls into several units with their chief nuclei in the State of Saxony, the ancient agglomeration of small States in Thuringia, Anhalt and the Province of Saxony, and Upper and Lower Lusatia on the eastern border.

In the Northern Lowlands, the southern limit of the dukedom of Saxony is still traceable in the map of 1790 and the same line appears in 1818. It is the southern limit of Low German dialects and of the Nordic racial type, as well as being a cultural divide. The dukedom of Saxony early fell into two parts, each of which was culturally, though not politically, a unit. Westphalia did not emerge as a political unit until created as a new province of Prussia, combining a number of interlocked territories, although with a common cultural heritage. *Niedersachsen* or Lower Saxony is a real cultural unit, although in this sense it includes Schleswig-Holstein and western Mecklenburg. Its traditional nucleus is the State, under various names, finally emerging as the province of Hanover with its capital in Hanover. These two areas, Westphalia and Lower Saxony, are distinct, in their religion, the one Catholic, the other Protestant, in the form of their settlements, their house types, and their folk-lore. The independent political units of the Weser Uplands are allied to both, but more decisively with Lower Saxony. In the lower Rhinelands, the boundary between the two new provinces of Westphalia and Rhineland was a very old one, and separated areas with marked cultural contrasts, although these have been considerably obscured in the economic sense since the modern growth of industry and population in this region, especially in the Ruhr.

East of the Elbe and the Saale there is little to be said, for the medieval units were absorbed into Prussia and adopted as provinces in 1815.

The last hundred years have brought profound changes in the structure of society. Geographical specialization of function and mobility are the key-notes to the new regional orientations that arise from these changes. The increase in the functions of the State means that its political divisions have a great variety of new functions devolved upon them, a fact that makes the existence of scattered territories a serious hindrance to efficient organization and service. Further, circulations and general relations are more closely knit geographically and often cut across these divisions. The broad pattern of the new distributions and space relationships is evidenced by four sets of facts—the distribution of population, of agriculture, of industry and of commerce. These will be sketched very briefly so as to present the broad basic picture to the problem as a whole, before describing the individual regions in more detail.

III. The Distribution of Population (Fig. 13)

The population of Germany in 1939, including the Saar, was 69·6 millions on an area of 472,605 square kilometres, a density of 147 persons per square kilometre. Of this total one-third lives in rural areas and two-thirds in urban areas, rural and urban being defined as parishes with below and over 2,000 inhabitants. Nearly two-fifths of the total population live in towns with under 100,000 inhabitants, and just over a quarter in towns with over 100,000 inhabitants. The main features of this geographical distribution are shown on Fig. 13.

It will be noticed at once that there are two broad belts of high density of both rural and urban populations. These may be called the Mid-German belt, running west–east right across the centre of Germany; and the Rhineland belt, running north–south across the west of Germany, the two converging in north-west Germany and the Low Countries. Consider each of these belts separately for a moment with regard to the so-called rural population. It will be evident that high rural densities must be due above all to the proportion of the land that is under cultivation and to the productivity of farming, and these in turn depend mainly on the fertility of the soil and the nearness to great consuming markets—namely, the big urban centres. Of secondary, but also of very great importance, are the facts that many places with under 2,000 people have many of their inhabitants

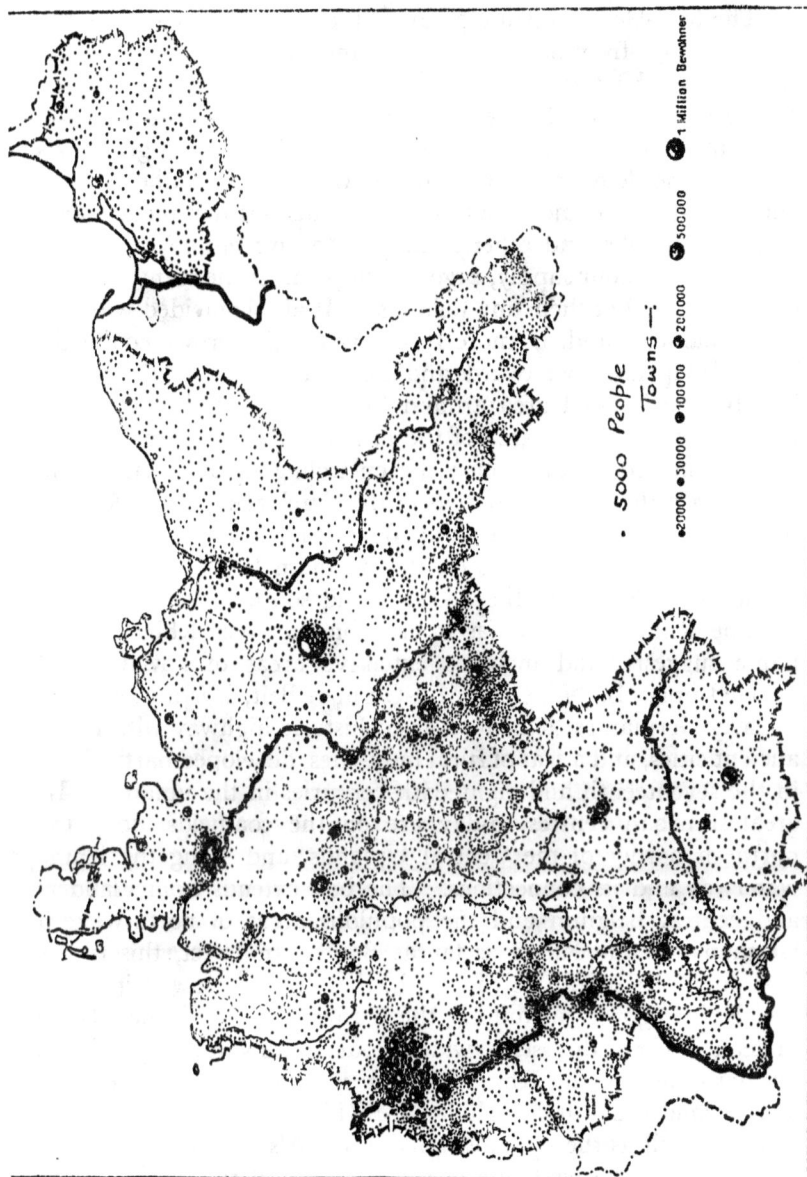

FIG. 13.—The Distribution of Population—(After Scheu.)

engaged in industry, and many places near cities include the homes of people working in office or factory in the cities.

The Mid-German Belt is a part of the great belt that stretches across Europe from northern France and Britain to south Russia. It includes the fertile soils of the *Börde* zone that lie on the northern border of the Central Uplands, though such soils also occur in these uplands to the south. This has been a great axis of historic settlement and movements with old-established towns, and with domestic industries in the uplands—at first metal working, then textiles and other industries to give employment to a large skilled labour supply, eager to supplement the scanty returns of the poor soil of their tiny holdings. It also coincided with the great coalfields and, in more recent years, the brown-coalfields. The belt tapers out westwards and is linked up with the Rhineland belt by the isolated area around Osnabrück. It broadens out in the great populous area of the middle Elbe basin and Silesia, and extends south to include the encircling uplands, stretching right across the upland frontiers of the Erzebirge and the Sudetes uplands without a break into Bohemia. Eastwards, beyond Upper Silesia, it continues on the northern border of the Carpathians in Poland to the Ukraine and south Russia.

The Rhineland Belt has its axis on the river Rhine, as the name suggests, and includes extensive areas of lowland and wooded uplands. Like the Mid-German Belt, it is a great area of early German settlement, a great historic highway with many ancient cities, and a seat of rural industries, developed particularly in the seventeenth and eighteenth centuries in the uplands. Its greatest urban centres to-day are on the coalfields along the northern border of the Central Uplands, and along the Rhine waterway and its connections. The belt extends from Flanders and central Belgium and the populous areas of north-western Germany up the Rhine as far as Bonn. In effect, this is one vast populous area. To the south, there is a narrow strip along the Rhine gorge including the eastern part of the Rhine plateau. Then this strip widens out southwards beyond the southern edge of the Rhine Plateau in the Upper Rhinelands. This second great area includes the Rhine plain from Bingen to Basel, as well as the uplands flanking it—Alsace, the Vosges, the Palatinate on the west side of the Rhine, and the Neckar basin (Wurtemberg), Hesse and Baden on the east side of the Rhine. It ends in the south against the Alps, including the populous area of Switzerland.

These two belts, the Mid-German and the Rhineland belts, included the most populous areas a hundred years ago—namely, the areas of handicraft industries and machine-driven industries, using the running water in swift flowing upland streams—and the fertile lowlands along the Rhine and along the *Börde* zone. Here, too, were the great historic highways and the chief cities. In the Mid-German Belt, the occurrence of coal and brown-coal, and the proximity of minerals in the adjacent uplands : and, in the Rhineland Belt, the great waterway of the Rhine, that allows these materials to be brought upstream, have greatly furthered modern industrial development and the clustering of urban populations around the medieval cities.

There is a marked concentration of towns with over 10,000 inhabitants in these belts. If we consider those towns only that are dominantly industrial, with over a half of their people dependent on industry, this fact is even more striking, for there then stand out three areas of town clusters : Rhineland-Westphalia, the middle Elbe basin, and the South-west. The middle Elbe area has extensions from Magdeburg to Berlin, and eastwards to Lusatia and northern Silesia, and westwards into Thuringia. The intermediate belt between the middle Elbe and the Rhine has a sprinkling of smaller industrial towns, including as its chief centres Hanover and Brunswick. The South-west has marked concentrations along the Rhine itself, notably the cluster around Frankfurt and Mainz at the northern end of the plain, with Mannheim, Karlsruhe, Strasbourg and Basel to the south, and a marked cluster in Baden and Wurtemberg. Apart from these industrial areas, there are large cities, isolated, as it were, in the midst of relatively thinly peopled rural land. These are Munich, Breslau, Stettin, Königsberg, Bremen, Hamburg and Kiel, and, biggest of all, Berlin. Towns with less than half their people dependent on industry (that is, those that are mainly seats of service for their surroundings) are evenly distributed over the land.

These two populous belts are separated by more thinly peopled, and predominantly agricultural areas. A great area of medium density, triangular in shape, with its southern base against the Alps, and its apex in the lower Weser uplands, has an average density of 40 to 70 persons per square kilometre, and covers the heart of the Central Uplands between the two populous belts. Within this great area there are patches of higher density around the cities of Erfurt, Würzburg, Nürnberg, Augsburg and Munich. To the north of the Mid-German Belt the

thinly peopled zone of the Northern Lowland has a rural density
of only 20 to 40 persons per square kilometre. Higher densities,
however, are found in the northern coastlands and in the north-
west against Holland.

IV. GENERAL ECONOMIC STRUCTURE (Fig. 14).

In 1939 the occupations of the Reich were as follows :

Percentage,
1939.

1. Agriculture and Forestry   .   .   .   18
2. Industry and Handicrafts   .   .   .   41
3. Trade and Transport   16
4. Public Service   12
5. Independent Means without occupation.   13

Three facts may be stated as keys to the economic structure
of modern Germany and the revolutionary changes in its development since 1871.   First, the numbers fully engaged in agriculture
have increased from 7 to 9⅓ million (1882–1933), while the
numbers dependent on agriculture (workers and their dependants)
decreased from 16 million to 13·6 million (40 per cent. to 21 per
cent. of the total population), although agricultural production has
increased enormously.   Second, there has been a tremendous
increase in the numbers of persons employed in industry, though
the proportion dependent on industry has increased little—indica-
ing an almost complete change in industrial structure through
the advent of the factory, large units, and mechanized processes.
Third, the accompanying concentration of population in cities
has reversed the geographical distribution as between rural (in
parishes with under 2,000 inhabitants) and urban (both in small
towns with 2,000 to 100,000 inhabitants and large cities with
over 100,000 inhabitants).   In 1875, 61 per cent. lived in rural
areas, and 33 per cent. in small towns and 6·3 per cent. in large
cities.   In 1925, 35 per cent. was classed as rural, with 37·6 per
cent. in rural towns and 27 per cent. in large cities.   Thus, there
has been a reversal of population distribution as between the
open countryside and the large city.

These facts mean that (1) Germany is the greatest single
industrial nation in Europe (outside Russia), with the greatest
production of the bases of modern industry—coal and iron ;
(2) Germany has prodigiously transformed and increased her
agricultural output, and under normal conditions produces about
85 per cent. of her own food requirements, the remaining 15 per

cent. being relatively small, but nevertheless a vital proportion, essential to her national life (grains and fats and tropical products) ; (3) Germany's output and demand for goods and services is primarily concerned with the home market, but foreign markets are equally vital—markets in the border-states in Europe, and markets overseas in tropical lands, and especially in the countries of East-Central Europe and the Balkans

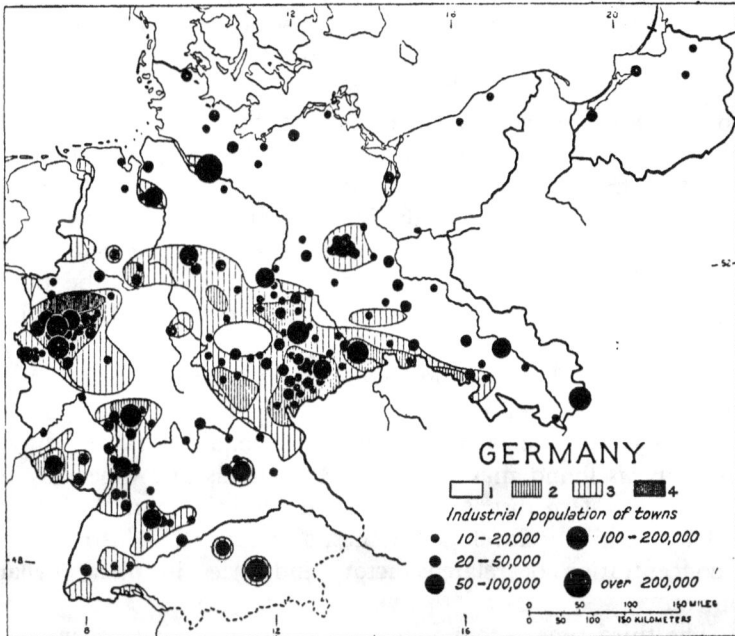

FIG. 14.—Distribution of Industrial and Agricultural Occupations (1925), prepared by *Institut für Konjunkturforschung* and reproduced by M. Pfannschmidt in *Standort, Landesplanung, Baupolitik,* 1932. (After *American Geographical Review,* 1938.)
Key to areas : 1, agricultural ; 2, exclusively industrial ; 3, dominantly industrial ; 4, Ruhr.

that primarily produce agricultural products in exchange for industrial products.

The extent of the main agricultural and industrial areas in Germany is shown on Fig. 14. This is in large measure a replica of the distribution of population. The area in which agricultural occupations are dominant covers one-half of the total area and contains about a quarter of the total population. It corresponds with the areas of lowest population density with under 80 persons to the square kilometre. In these areas from 50 per cent. to

60 per cent. (including the small towns) of the entire population is dependent on agriculture, and a similar proportion lives in rural areas, i.e. villages with under 2,000 inhabitants.

In the remaining half of the country, the industrial exceeds the agricultural population.   Here, too, the density of population exceeds 100 to the square kilometre and here are concentrated the majority of the great cities and the towns.   But within it the density of population and the economic structure varies widely.

Thus, we may recognize four types of economic area.

The first type has an average rural density (about 30 to 35 persons per square kilometre), and a high proportion in industry and commerce, these two together giving occupation to three times as many people as agriculture ; while about 40 per cent. of the population is rural, the remainder is in towns. This type is found especially in the Mid-German Belt, from Münster to the industrialized upland districts of the Sudetes in Silesia.   Its widest extent is found in the middle Elbe basin where it extends from the Elbe river as far west as the Thuringian Forest.

The second type is also highly industrialized, but it has a high agricultural density (40 to 50 per square kilometre), a fact which is to be associated with its exceptionally small holdings. This type is found mainly in the Rhinelands and especially in the south-western districts.   It is characterized by a close rural settlement, highly developed domestic handicraft industries, and a concentration of related factory industries in many urban centres.

The third type is found in the highly industrialized areas in which there is an average density of agricultural population, but agriculture is completely overshadowed by industry and commerce.   These are the great industrial areas of Germany, the Lower Rhinelands with its chief nucleus in the Ruhr ; Saxony ; the Saar ; and the small section of the Upper Silesian area which lies in Germany.   These areas together accommodate some 15 million people, nearly one-quarter of the total population of the Reich, on one-tenth of the area.   The Ruhr is completely urbanized, with a total population of some $4\frac{1}{2}$ millions.   Saxony is a land in which industrial towns are scattered in a rural countryside ; the same type of economic structure and population distribution is found in the coalfields of Northern France and Flanders.   Upper Silesia is an exclusively industrial area.   In the Saar, on the other hand, mining and industry are interspersed with farming, and the miner often has a bit of land which he works as a subsidiary occupation.

Lastly, the great city forms a distinct entity in its social and economic structure. Most of the cities are intimately bound up, in historical development as in present functions, with the lands which surround them ; others are outgrowths of modern industry. Still others are great historic cities placed in the midst of thinly peopled areas, whose activities they integrate, but which certainly did not call them into being. All such cities perform special services of a national character. The chief of them are Berlin, and the lower Weser and Elbe areas, with their capitals in Bremen and Hamburg. Of somewhat similar character are Breslau and Munich.

V.   AGRICULTURE AND AGRICULTURAL REGIONS

Turning to the character and extent of the chief types of farming, we may first note the size of holdings (Fig. 15). Holdings of under 5 hectares (one hectare equals about 2·5 acres), take up 11·5 per cent. of the farmed areas and are dominant throughout western Germany. On the other hand, large holdings and estates with over a hundred hectares take up 20 per cent. of the farm area and are dominant in eastern Germany, east of the Elbe and the upper Oder. The Junker or large landowner on these great estates depends upon the hired labour of a rural proletariat. With a high birth-rate among its rural folk, a lack of non-rural occupations, and the spread of large-scale mechanized farming, this has been a main reservoir for the urban centres. Intermediate holdings (5 to 50 hectares) are dominant between these two main areas throughout central Germany. The very small holding of less than 5 hectares is normally not adequate to meet all the requirements of the farmer and his family, and he usually has another string to his bow, working for another peasant with a larger holding, engaging in a handicraft, or working in a factory. The intermediate-sized holding of from 5 to 50 hectares, which is the type held by the typical peasant farmer, provides sufficient for the livelihood of the farmer and his family and some outside labour at harvest time.

Mixed farming everywhere predominates, and no farms depend exclusively on grain production. Even the largest farms of the great grain-growing lands in the *Börde* zone draw at least a third to a half of their income from the sale of animal products,

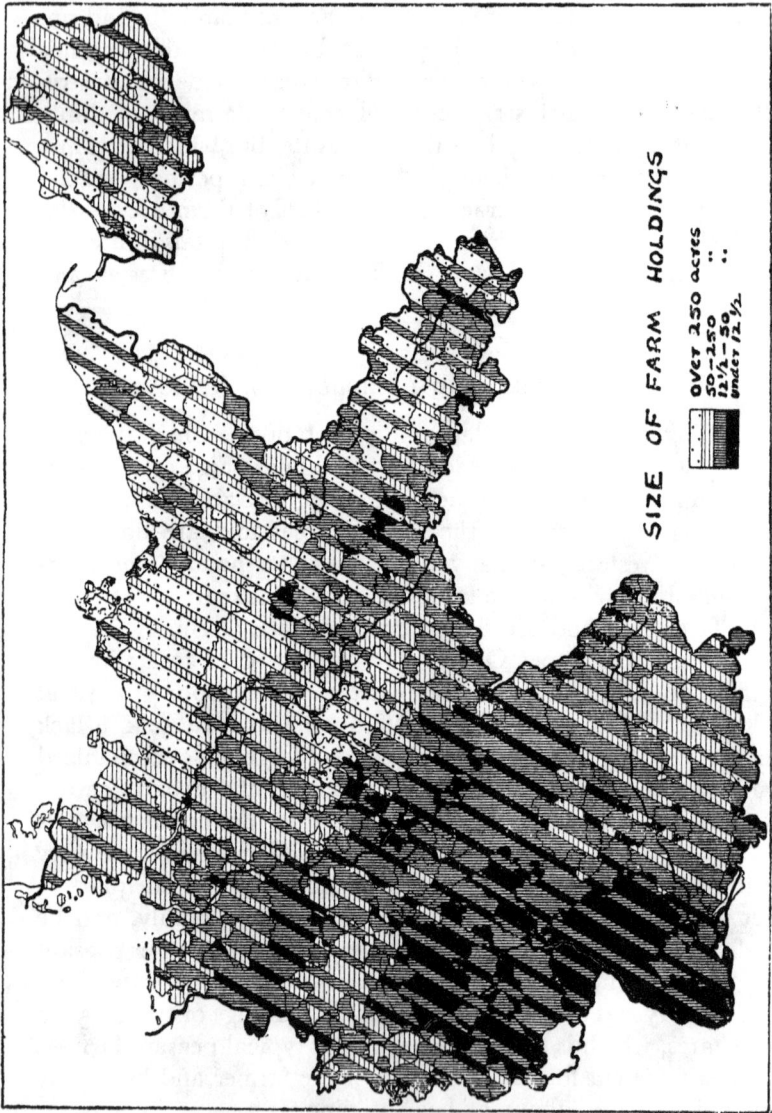

SIZE OF FARM HOLDINGS

Over 250 acres
50–250   ,,
12½–50   ,,
under 12½

Fig. 15.—Size of Farm Holdings.
(After Niehaus.)

while those depending on the sale of livestock products only
carry an intensive arable cultivation on about a third of their
land.   For the Reich as a whole two-thirds of the agricultural
production is derived from animals and animal products, and
one-third from crops.   It is according to the proportions of crops
and animal production and sales that the classification of
agricultural regions shown on Fig. 16 has been based.

The chief livestock farming areas coincide with the grassland

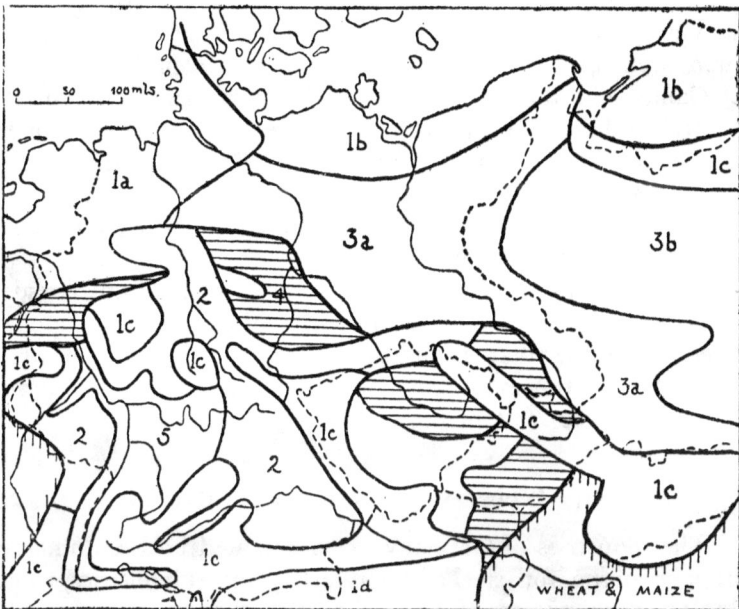

Fig. 16.—Agricultural Regions.
(After Niehaus.)

1a, North-western Lowlands : dairying and beef production ; pastures, hay, rye and oats, forage
crops ; small holdings. 1b, Baltic Uplands : rolling land ; products as 1a ; large holdings and estates.
1c, Low Mountains and Foothills : dairying, pasture, forest. 1d, High Alps. 2, Hilly Country : rye
and oats, potatoes, livestock. 3a, Plains and Rolling Land : rye, potatoes, livestock, with forest and
marsh dominant. 3b, Plains and Rolling Land : arable land dominant (over 70 per cent. of total
area) with wheat and barley subsidiary to rye. 4. (Horizontal lines), Plains and Rolling Land : wheat,
barley, sugar beet, livestock, over 70 per cent. of total area under arable land. 5, River Valleys and
Hill Land in South-western Germany ; wine, fruits, and grain ; very small holdings.

belts, the north-western lowland, the Baltic uplands and the
south Bavarian plateau, each having its distinctive type of
economy.   The high plateaus of the Central Uplands have
a heavy rainfall and are largely forested, and farming is centred
on the growth of quick-growing crops (rye and potatoes), and
the use of meadow and grass for the production of butter and
cheese for sale to distant markets.

The areas which draw the bulk of their income from crop sales are mainly in the arable lands. Throughout the hill and basin country of central Germany from the lower Weser in the north to the Alps in the south the basins are mainly arable farming areas with small holdings, which often do not meet the requirements of the farmer and his family. On the other hand, in the valleys of south-western Germany, where it is dry, and the summers long and hot and winters mild, a variety of crops for sale is grown. By far the most important of these is, of course, the vine, together with tobacco and hops and orchards. But the main areas of crop production and sales are in the Northern Lowlands and the *Börde* zone on the northern border of the Central Uplands. East of the Elbe, rye and potatoes dominate on the poorer sandy soils, while in the *Börde* zone, the greatest belt of commercialized farming in Germany, wheat, sugar beet and the production of stall-fed stock and dairy produce (especially milk near the cities) are dominant.

The southern half of Germany, south of a line from Dresden to the Ruhr is, on balance, an importer of certain food supplies, especially grain, potatoes and pigs. The principal surplus areas are in the north-western lowlands, the *Börde*, and the rye and potato provinces east of the Elbe.

VI. INDUSTRY AND INDUSTRIAL REGIONS

The industries of Germany are dominated by the numerous branches of the iron, steel and non-ferrous metal industries, which employ over a quarter of the total employed population ; and by the textile and clothing industries, which employ about one-fifth. These two groups of industries thus together account for about one-half of the industrial population. Mining and quarrying account for 12 per cent. and the food and drink industries together with the building trades for about a quarter. Of all these industries, about one-third of the occupied persons are in industries that are specially localized in particular areas, because of either an early historical development or of the bulky materials they handle. The remaining two-thirds are related to the distribution of population and transport facilities and are distributed proportionally to these. In consequence, the localized industries form the basis of the pyramid of the occupational structure and give rise to marked regional variations in the economic structure of the predominantly industrial areas of the

country. Let us note quite broadly the distribution of these
more highly localized industries, confining our attention to the
production and distribution of coal, iron ore, power, the iron
and steel industries, the textile industries, and the chemical,
glass, paper and leather industries.

The distribution of mineral resources is shown in Fig. 17.
Coal production amounts to about 150 million tons in normal
years (as in 1928). The chief seat of production is in the Ruhr

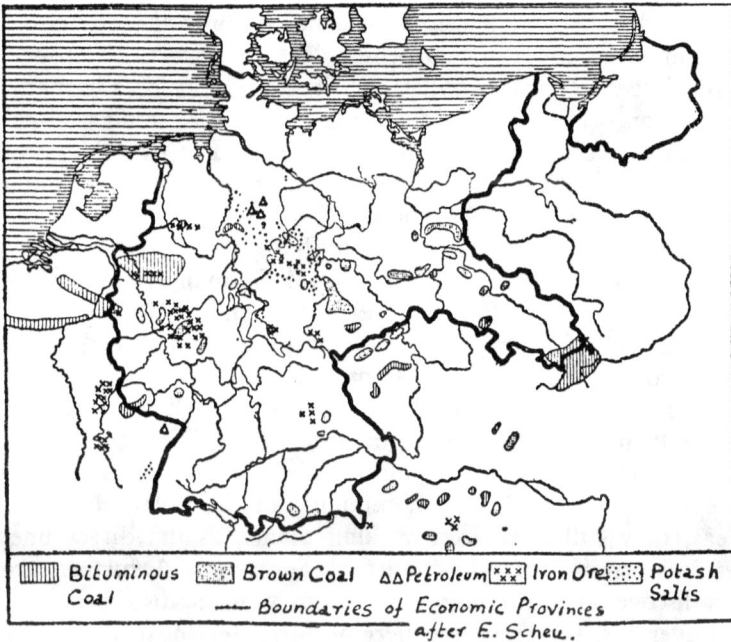

Bituminous Coal   Brown Coal   ▲▲Petroleum ✕✕✕ Iron Ore   Potash Salts
—— Boundaries of Economic Provinces
after E. Scheu.

FIG. 17.—Mineral Resources.
(After Vogel.)

industrial area, which produces three-quarters of Germany's
bituminous coal production. About a quarter comes from Upper
Silesia (20 million tons) and the Saar (10 million tons) together.
Apart from these three areas, there are several very small fields
scattered along the northern border of the Central Uplands,
linked up with the chain of coalfields that extends from Upper
Silesia through the Ruhr to central Belgium and northern France.

Lignite or brown coal, with a production reaching 165 million
tons in 1928, equalled bituminous coal in tonnage in 1937,
though not in heat value. Brown coal is a low-grade fuel inter-

mediate between coal and peat. It occurs in thick deposits near to the surface beneath the rich farmlands of the *Börde* zone on the northern edge of the Central Uplands. It is obtained from vast quarries and the material is deprived of its water and waste for the production of briquettes ; or it is fed direct as a fuel into furnaces for the generation of electricity and for the manufacture of chemicals. It is also distilled by low-temperature carbonization processes for the production of tar, oil and chemicals. The great advance in the utilization of lignite during and since the last war has been responsible for a new industrial revolution in Germany, the importance of which does not seem to be properly appreciated in this country. If it were not for Germany's production of synthetic oil from this source she would probably long ago have used up existing oil stocks. The two chief areas of production of lignite are the Lower Rhinelands in the funnel of low land south of Cologne on the west bank of the Rhine, and sufficiently near the Ruhr to have the closest economic relations with the latter ; and Central Germany in the middle Elbe basin around Leipzig and Halle and including Lower Lusatia. The former produces about 30 per cent. and the latter about 70 per cent. of the total production.

Iron ore is produced in the Sieg, Lahn and Dill valleys in the Rhine Plateau east of the Rhine and south of the Ruhr. Iron mining and working is very old-established in these areas, and, in spite of the difficulties of mining and the isolation of these areas, they still have iron-working plants, as the direct lineal descendants of their pre-industrial ancestors. A further area was discovered in the nineteenth century in the district between Hanover and the Harz and here at Salzgitter (near Brunswick) the new Göring works have been established. Before the last war, Germany's vast iron and steel production was based on the iron production of German Lorraine, that reached 40 million tons a year, so that Germany was then nearly three-quarters self-sufficing. Since 1918 Germany, deprived of these supplies, has been able to cover only a quarter of her needs from domestic sources. In order to diminish this dependence on foreign supplies domestic production was increased to some 11 million tons in 1938. Of this domestic production about a third comes from the Siegerland, a fifth from Peine-Salzgitter, a tenth from the Lahn-Dill area, and 8 per cent. from each of the Vogelsberg and Bavaria.

Non-ferrous metals are produced in very small quantities and

the bulk is imported.   Copper is mined in the Mansfeld district.
Zinc (70 per cent.) and lead (30 per cent.) are obtained in Upper
Silesia and the Rhine Plateau (25 and 40 per cent.), although
60 per cent. of the pre-1918 production in Upper Silesia was
ceded to Poland by the Versailles Treaty.   Germany is rich in
salts, the mining of which contributed to the development of the
chemical industries in the 'sixties and after.   The chief are the
potash salts that occur in a belt around the Harz, this whole
area yielding nearly three-quarters of Germany's vast production,
that has favoured both the development of chemical industries
and the supply of Germany's poor lands with artificial fertilizers.
Rock salt is mined in the Magdeburg area near the Harz together
with potash salts, but the chief seat of production is in the Neckar
basin and near Berchtesgaden.

The power for the industrial and domestic life of Germany is
drawn mainly from three sources—coal, lignite and running
water.   Especially notable are the dependence of Central Germany (the Province of Saxony, and the States of Saxony and
Thuringia) on lignite ; the Province of Rhineland by a third
on lignite, and the Province of Westphalia almost entirely on
coal and gas from the Ruhr'; while the southern States depend
almost entirely on the hydro-electric plants in the Bavarian Alps.
Berlin and Brandenburg draw their power in equal quantities
from coal and lignite.   The chief hydro-electric plants are
situated in the Bavarian Alps although other plants are in construction, as on the Saale in Thuringia and the Mulde in Saxony.
The chief supplies of electricity, however, are derived from
centralized thermal (coal and lignite) plants, and networks of
transmission lines are to be found in the middle Elbe basin and
Lower Lusatia, which supply Berlin, the Lower Rhinelands, the
middle Weser lands, the Frankfurt area, and the upper Rhine.

The distribution of the extractive and heavy industries and
of the manufacturing industries is shown on Figs. 18 and 19.
The chief seats of crude iron and steel production and rolling
mills in Western Europe are situated in the Ruhr and in Lorraine, each producing about 10 million tons of pig iron.   Since
1919, having lost the Lorraine supply, four-fifths of the crude
iron and steel is produced in the Ruhr, while secondary areas
are located in the Sieg, Lahn and Dill valleys, the Upper Silesian
coalfield and in the Salzgitter iron ore district.   The Ruhr
enjoys the supreme advantage of good water transport by the
Rhine, by which iron ores are imported.   Upper Silesia suffers

in that its coal is not suited to coking, it has no local ores, and
its water transport facilities are inadequate. Secondary centres
of production are found in the northern ports, based normally
upon imported ores and English coal, which form the basis of
their shipbuilding industries.

The older seats of iron and metal working have to some
extent maintained themselves partly by using local iron, partly

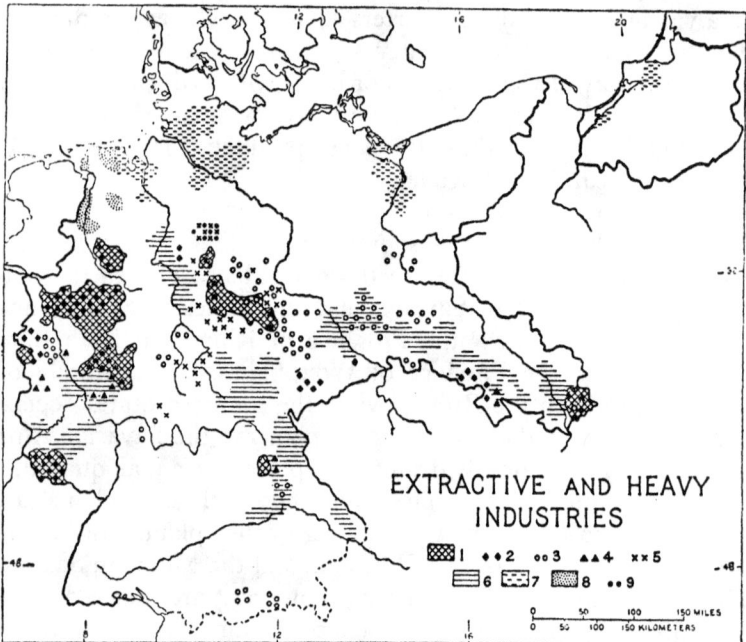

Fig. 18.—Distribution of Extractive and Heavy Industries.
(Based on occupations by *Kreise*.)

1, heavy industries ; 2, coal ; 3, lignite (brown coal) ; 4, iron ore ; 5, salt ; 6, quarrying ;
7, coastal industries (marine engineering, shipbuilding, treatment of imported products, etc.) ; 8, peat ;
9, oil. Adapted from von Geldern Crispendorf (after *American Geographical Review*, 1938).

by importing it, and have concentrated on the production of
goods of high value and great variety, which demand skilled
labour. Thus the old workshop industry is retained in the metal
(cutlery) working of Solingen and Remscheid ; the Sauerland
retains its production of small iron wares, especially wire products ;
and varied iron-working industries, notably ironmongery, are
carried on in Saxony and Thuringia.

The great bulk of the iron and steel manufacturing industries
are located on or near the seats of iron and steel production ;

while a large number are widely distributed in the chief cities. The manufacture of rolling stock is situated at the great railway foci, though the greatest centres are in the Lower Rhinelands, and in Berlin, the biggest city and railroad focus in the Reich. The two other chief centres for the production of railway stock are Hanover and Kassel. The manufacture of agricultural machinery is located in relation to the consuming market, namely, the agricultural regions of the middle Elbe basin (Magdeburg, Hanover, Leipzig), Silesia (Breslau), the Lower Rhinelands

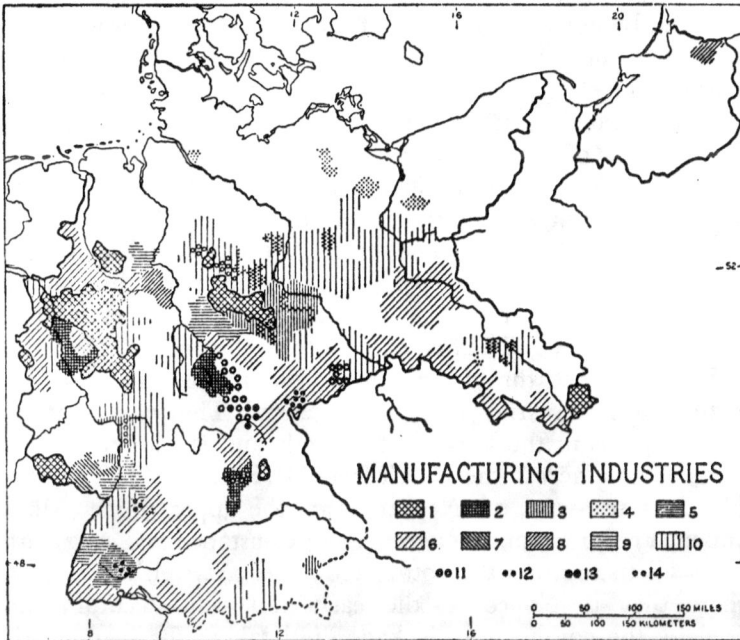

FIG. 19.—Distribution of Manufacturing Industries.

1, heavy industries; 2, iron and metal working; 3, chemicals; 4, electrical; 5, optical, etc.; 6, leather, boots and shoes; 8, wood, paper; 9, tobacco; 10, mixed industries; 11, toys; 12, musical instruments; 13, basket work; 14, food preserves. Adapted from von Geldern Crispendorf (after *American Geographical Review*, 1938).

(Düsseldorf, Cologne), but not in the Ruhr area itself. The manufacture of vehicles (bicycles and automobiles) is located usually in the place where the founder of the firm started his business in a number of medium-sized and large cities.

The great range of industries producing machinery, tools and apparatus, is concentrated in the Lower Rhinelands, Saxony and Berlin. In the Lower Rhinelands, concentration is upon goods which are needed in the heavy industries (Essen, Mülheim).

The fine machinery, tool and instruments industries are especially characteristic of the whole of west Saxony and part of Thuringia, a fact which is to be related to the skill of a large population, which, in the latter half of the nineteenth century, was available for factory work. Moreover, the fact that the textile industries are mainly located in this area has attracted the manufacture of textile machinery. Thus, while the Lower Rhinelands specialize on bulky goods, which use larger supplies of semi-manufactured materials, and cater for the heavy industries, in the Saxon-Thuringian area the concentration is upon fine machine work. It should be noted, however, that these finer industries are found in most of the great cities, especially Berlin, which is the chief centre of the electrical industries. The machine industries of the ports are related to marine engineering. In south Germany the chief centres of these light engineering industries (machinery, machine tools, and electrical apparatus) are Frankfurt, Nürnberg, Mannheim, Stuttgart and Munich.

The textile industries come second to the iron and steel group in numbers occupied (20 per cent. together with the clothing industries.) They appear as the dominant industries in three areas in Germany. The first extends from the Sudetes Highlands in Silesia, thence through Saxony, west of the Elbe, and into north-eastern Bavaria (Hof), and central Thuringia (Erfurt). The second is in the Lower Rhinelands and is contiguous with a similar area across the Dutch frontier (Enschede). The third is in the south-west, the Neckar basin, the upper Rhine (Mühlhausen, Freiburg), and between Lake Constance and Augsburg.

In all these areas the cotton industries are well represented, where they developed in the early nineteenth century, fostered by the continental blockade, and taking the place of the earlier flax industry which was then decadent. The three chief areas are Saxony, the Lower Rhinelands and Wurtemberg. The woollen textile industries were first domiciled in the early Middle Ages in Flanders, Friesland and Münsterland ; and in the towns of the south (Regensburg, Augsburg). Under Frederick the Great they spread into the Sudetes highlands, depending upon local wool, of which Prussia had an export surplus till the middle of the nineteenth century. The chief centres to-day are in west Saxony and central Thuringia. In the north-west, the old domestic industry is now concentrated in factories mainly in the towns of Aachen and Düren. The south is to-day of very little importance. Through the competition of cotton the widespread flax industry was displaced in the eighteenth century. To-day, its remnants are associated with the cotton manufacturing areas. The chief are in Lusatia (Zittau and Lauban), and in the Sudetes in Western Silesia and in the extreme south-east corner of Saxony. The two chief seats of knitting and embroidery making, which is carried on as a domestic industry organized from the town centres, are Central Saxony (Chemnitz and Plauen), in a large number of villages and small towns around Stuttgart in Wurtemberg.

The chemical industries, though occupying a small number of workers relative to other industries, are of the greatest importance in the economic life of an industrialized country. Their development has been synonymous with that of modern chemistry and extends over less than a hundred years, really taking effective root in Germany in the 'seventies. The two chief fillips to development were the manufacture of artificial fertilizers and of artificial dyes. The production of photographic materials and pharmaceutical apparatus followed in the 'eighties. The opening of the twentieth century witnessed the extraction of nitrogen from the atmosphere. The distillation of lignite has formed the basis of this development. The heavy chemical industries—those concerned with the large-scale production of bulky products from bulky raw materials—are tied to the location of the raw materials or where they can be cheaply assembled by water. Thus, there are three main districts with vast modern plants— the Lower Rhinelands (on the coalfield and on the Rhine—e.g. the I.G. Farben Plant at Leverkusen) ; Central Germany, near to the lignite quarries and salt works, which provide both raw materials and power (fertilizers, explosives, pharmaceutical products, synthetic oil and rubber) ; and the upper Rhine area on the river front, e.g. I.G. Farben and other chemical plants at Ludwigshafen-Mannheim. The light chemical industries, producing consumer goods (as opposed to production goods in the heavy industries) such as pharmaceutical products, photographic supplies, soaps, perfumes, etc., are not tied down to their raw materials by considerations of transport costs. They are located for the most part in towns.

The glass and porcelain industries, like the iron workings, were widespread in the Middle Ages in the uplands near the supply of timber, sands and clays. They began to be attracted to the coalfields after 1800 and to the lignite fields after 1850. They are now highly localized since, pursued on a much larger scale, they require large quantities of fuel. The chief modern centres are now highly concentrated on the Ruhr, the Saar, and the lignite areas of Lusatia and Saxony, on the coalfields where they can draw at minimum costs the great supplies of heat required in large-scale processes. The porcelain industry only dates from the end of the eighteenth century in Germany, when local clays were used by two men in Thuringia, encouraged by the ruling prince of the State. In the early nineteenth century two other centres were established in the north-east of Bavaria and in Silesia and these three areas now produce all Germany's output.

The paper-making industry was formerly dependent on local timber and running water for both processing and power. The chief area in the nineteenth century was in the Erzgebirge in the upper courses of the many streams. To-day, nearly a half of the timber is imported, mainly from Bohemia via the Elbe, and coal is drawn from Zwickau and lignite from the fields to the north. Both water power and steam power are widely used to-day, and Saxony is still the chief area of paper production, occupying a quarter of the persons so employed in Germany. Paper-making and the printing industries, apart from the chief centre in Berlin, are also highly concentrated in Leipzig, and to a lesser extent in other great cities.

Leather tanning was formerly mainly concentrated in the Rhinelands, especially in Hesse, using local hides and the tannin from the acorns of the oak forests which are confined to western Germany. To-day, tannin extract is obtained from quebracho wood and about half the consumption of skins and hides is imported. Consequently, new centres have grown up at or near the ports, notably in Schleswig-Holstein. The boot and shoe industry which consumes about a quarter of the leather production is located in two areas, in the south-west, in Wurtemberg (the town of Pirmasens in the Palatinate has 14,000 workers in these occupations alone), and a smaller area in Saxony and Thuringia.

The remaining industries are not markedly localized, but are widely distributed in relation to the distribution of population. The prominence of any one area is to be attributed to economic factors and not to the necessity of eliminating the high transport cost of bulky raw materials. This is true, for example, of the clothing industry and the manufacture of foods and drinks. The distribution of the latter is a replica of the distribution of population. There are, however, exceptions. The sugar beet industry is closely tied up with the areas of beet production. Cigar making is characteristic of the tobacco-producing areas in Baden and the Palatinate. This general principle holds good for the paper industries, wood working (with a special concentration in the upland areas of Thuringia, the Black Forest and Saxony), clothing, foods and drinks, building trades and utility services. Two-thirds of all the industrial occupations come into this general category.

VII. COMMERCE

The interchange of commodities as from one point of the Reich to another, across the frontiers and to and from the ports, both sea and river ports, is reflected in the main traffic flows by water, rail and road. These are shown on Figs. 20, 21, 22, 23, 24. Road and rail maps reveal the closest network and the densest traffic in the industrial areas of Rhineland-Westphalia and Saxony, and, thirdly, in and around Berlin. The first two are, in effect, the most densely populated parts of the Mid-German Belt that extends färther east to Silesia. A second belt lies in the Rhinelands and extends south to the Swiss frontier. There is, in general, a marked concentration of traffic around the cities which are the outstanding centres of radial routes. The modern *Autobahnen* (Fig. 24), it may be noticed, are so constructed as to feed, but not to add to the congestion of traffic in, the big centres of population. Thus, in general, they skirt the big cities to which they are connected by side roads.

Railways carry the bulk of the traffic, both goods and passenger (Figs. 22, 23). Waterways (Fig. 20), on the other hand, are limited to a few main arteries, with collection and distribution by rail, or to a smaller degree by road, from riverside ports. The Rhine (taking 2,500-ton barges to Strasbourg), the Weser (taking 1,000-ton barges to Minden),[1] the Elbe (taking 600-ton barges to Prague in Bohemia), and the Oder (taking 500-ton barges to Kosel, which is now connected direct by a new canal to the Upper Silesian coalfield) are the main north–south navigable rivers.[2] The Rhine system carries 60 per cent. of the river-borne

[1] The river Werra is being regularized above this town to near Eisenach, and improvements farther upstream to Merkers, a potash-producing district, are planned. It is projected to build a deep canal from the head of the Werra to the Main, thus linking up with the main Danube canal, which is now nearing completion. This, however, is still a matter of the future.

[2] In progress are the Saarbrücken-Mannheim canal for 1,200-ton barges, the Bamberg-Kelheim canal linking the Main and Danube along the line of the old Ludwigs canal (which was only available for 120-ton barges), and the canal connection between Halle and Leipzig, that will bring the latter into direct contact with the Elbe and Mittelland canal systems. The Main is navigable to Würzburg and the Neckar to Plochingen.

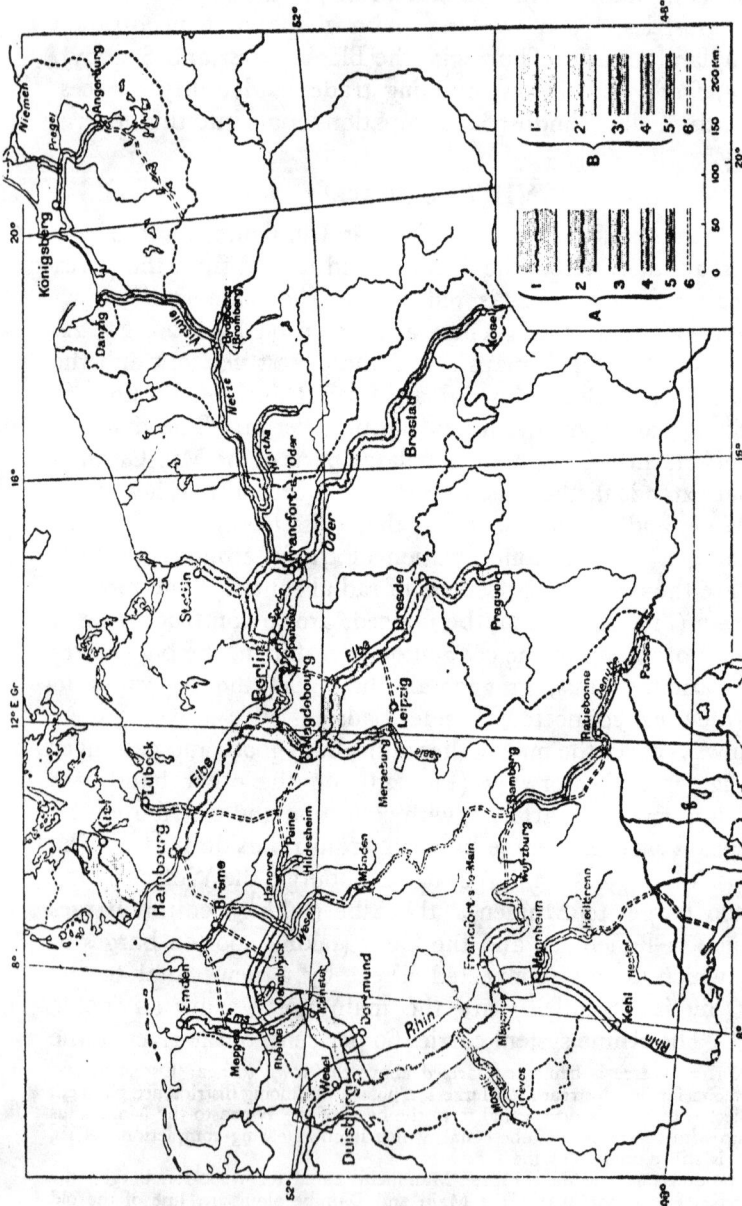

FIG. 20.—Canal and River Goods Traffic.

(After De Martonne, 1930.)

A. Rivers.   B. Canals.   Importance of Traffic; 1 and 1': over 10 million tons, 2 and 2': over 5 million tons, 3 and 3': over 2 million tons, 4 and 4': 1 million tons, 5 and 5': less than 1 million tons. 6, River improvement projects, 6', Canal projects.   Note that the Mittelland Canal is now completed to beyond Magdeburg.   The Neckar is now navigable beyond Heilbronn to Plochingen and there is a new canal from Kosel on the Oder to Gleiwitz.

traffic and the Elbe system 27 per cent. The Northern Lowland is well suited to the construction of canals from one river to another. A crossways of canals intersects at Berlin and links the Oder and the Elbe systems. The recently completed Mittelland canal, taking barges of about 1,000 tons, now links the Elbe with

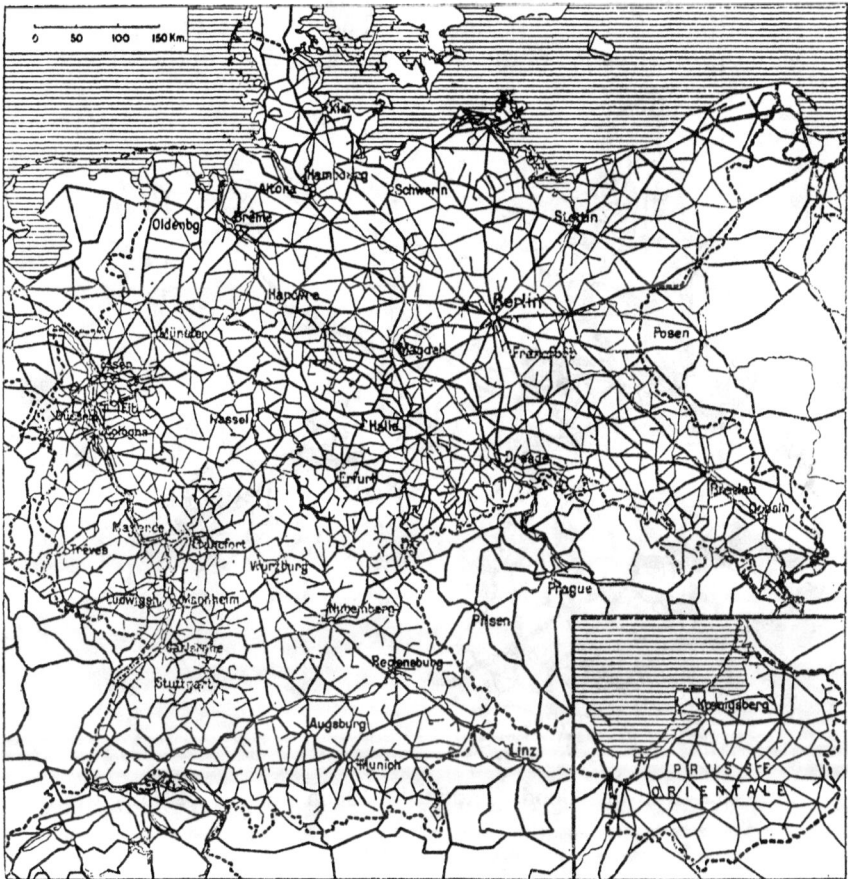

FIG. 21.—The Railways of Germany.
(After De Martonne, 1930.)
Only the main lines are shown outside Germany.

the Dortmund-Ems canal and so with the Ruhr and the Rhine. The total of water-borne traffic is about a quarter of the rail-borne traffic and 40 per cent. of the traffic of both consists of coal.

It is not necessary to our theme to discuss the overseas trade of Germany except in relation to the functions of the ports as

centres for the collection from and distribution to their hinterlands.   Here it may be noted that the Baltic ports were of great
importance in the Middle Ages for their trade with eastern Germany and western Russia and the Baltic lands, but to-day they
are completely dwarfed (though they are still important in the
aggregate) by the two ports of Hamburg and Bremen and the third
small North Sea port of Emden.   The last rose to importance
with the construction of the Dortmund-Ems canal in the 'nineties,

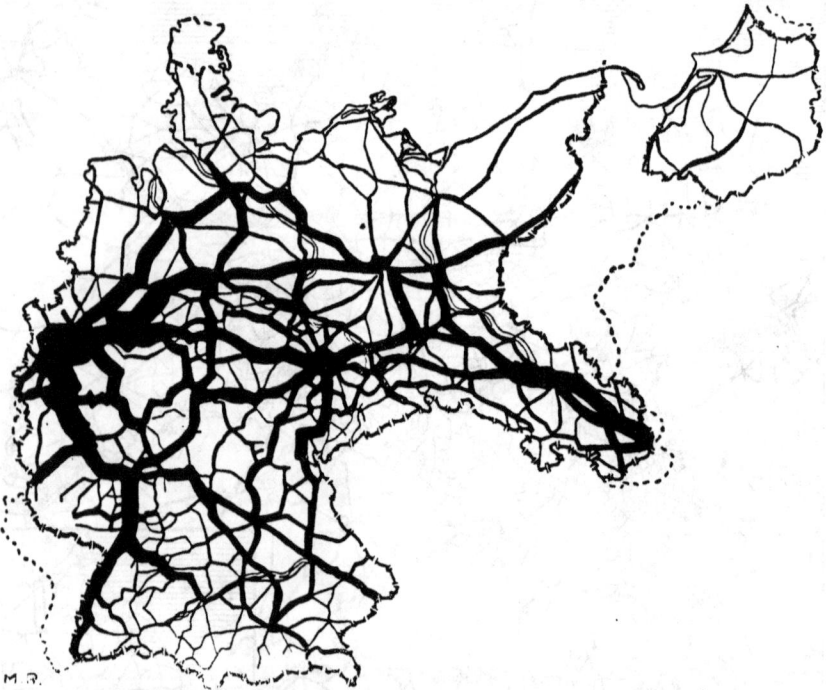

FIG. 22.—Railway Goods Traffic, based on number of daily trains,
1925.
(After Pfannschmidt.)

that was designed as a feeder to the Ruhr industrial area to
compete with the Rhine waterway, whose traffic is mainly handled
by Rotterdam.   Hamburg handles well over a half of the foreign
trade of Germany and its main hinterland, excluding the
numerous scattered places in and outside Germany that it serves,
is the Elbe basin, upstream to the frontier, with Schleswig-
Holstein, and Berlin-Brandenburg, all of which are connected
by a good system of waterways.   Bremen has as its hinterland
the Weser basin, which is now connected with the Ruhr and the

Elbe via the Mittelland canal. The Weser, however, is an inferior waterway as compared with the Elbe. Moreover, the lower Weser is physically much more difficult for navigation than the lower Elbe. Consequently, Bremen has used its outport of Bremerhaven for large sea-going vessels and its inland connections are predominantly by rail, as opposed to the large proportion of Hamburg's inland traffic that is carried by river barge. It is not surprising, therefore, that, specializing on lighter cargoes, its

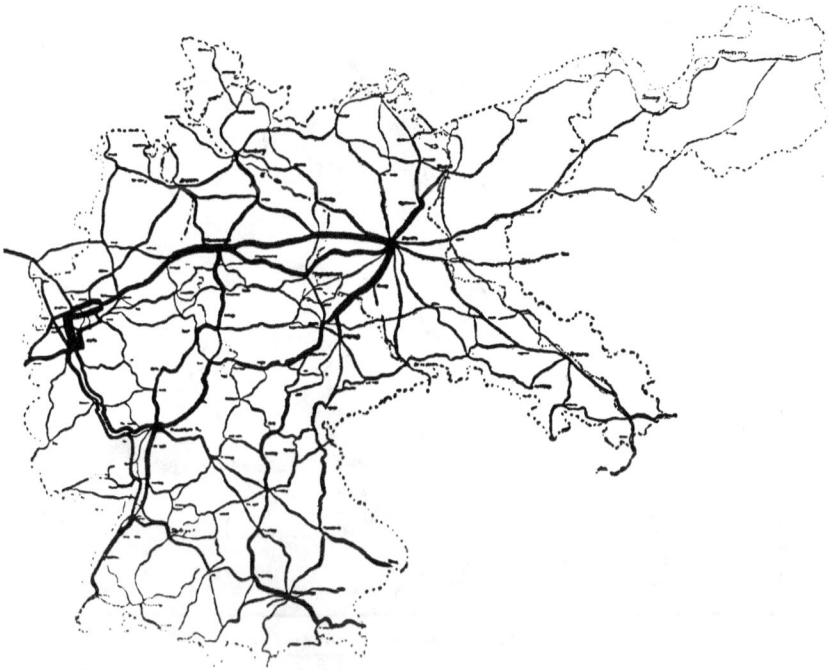

Fig. 23.—Railway Passenger Traffic, based on number of
daily trains, 1925.
(After Pfannschmidt.)

share of Germany's foreign trade (in tonnage) amounts to little more than a tenth. About 6 per cent. of the total tonnage is handled by Emden. Thus two-thirds of Germany's foreign trade is handled by the three North Sea ports. A chief concern of the Reich government has been to help these ports to compete with the ports of the Low Countries which are better situated to deal with the Rhineland traffic. In fact, the whole of western Germany lies in the hinterland of Rotterdam for the great bulk of heavy

cargoes going up and down the Rhine—iron, upstream, and
much smaller quantities of grain, oil, timber and coal, downstream ; and of Antwerp, especially (as far as Germany is concerned) for the export of iron and steel and manufactured goods
by rail, for Antwerp is one of the best equipped liner-traffic and
transit ports in Europe and is geographically better situated for
Atlantic traffic than the German ports. There is also a large
traffic between Antwerp and the French provinces of Alsace and

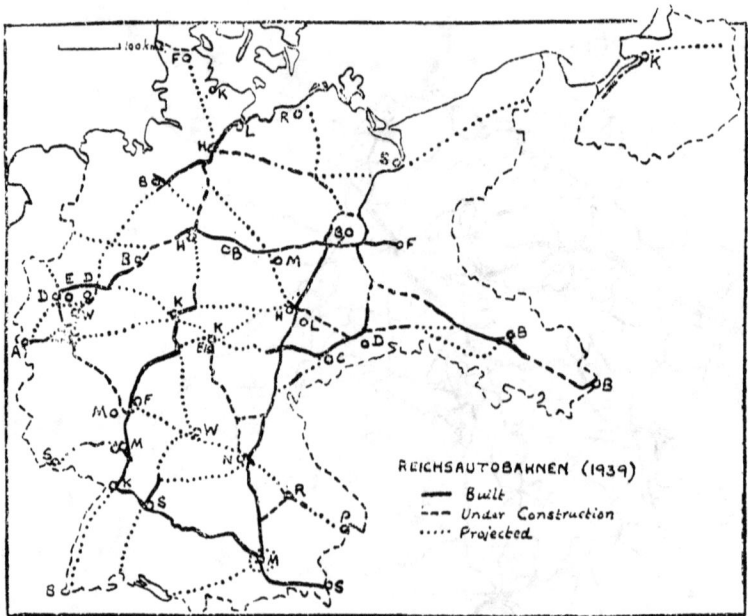

FIG. 24.—*Reichsautobahnen* (January, 1939).

Lorraine. This is effected not only by rail, but also by the
Rhine through Strasbourg, this port being treated by the French
as a seaport, by eliminating in 1919 the surtax that is charged at
all French ports on goods that have already been handled in
a foreign port.

The Rhine river ports are Duisburg-Ruhrort, Mannheim-
Ludwigshafen, and Strasbourg, to name but the chief. They
receive goods mainly from Rotterdam and serve as regional
distribution centres from river to rail and, in smaller degree, to
canal. The traffic of Duisburg-Ruhrort, the greatest river port in
Europe, is concerned exclusively with the Ruhr industrial area
that lies immediately east of it. But the other two serve wider

areas by rail in southern Germany (Mannheim), and eastern France (Alsace-Lorraine from Strasbourg), while both ports serve Switzerland. Basel is not regularly accessible by barge, but improvements have been made. Its imports have steadily increased in the inter-war years and reached nearly 2 million tons in the middle 'thirties. Through Strasbourg, Mannheim and Basel, Switzerland receives most of her coal, wheat and petrol. In south Germany, Mannheim is the chief gateway for the collection and distribution of supplies that go by the Rhine, although Hamburg and Bremen, especially the former, enjoy privileges in virtue of special freight rates which greatly reduce the factor of geographical distance.

The contribution of the Baltic ports is obviously relatively small—about one-third of the total tonnage of foreign trade. While Lübeck was the chief of German ports in the later Middle Ages, it has long been insignificant like its neighbours. The chief port to-day is Stettin at the mouth of the Oder, handling nearly a tenth of the overseas trade. The Oder basin, including Upper Silesia, is its main hinterland. It also has important canal connections with Berlin, though its service to the capital is decidedly small in comparison with that of Hamburg.

CHAPTER III

RHINELAND-WESTPHALIA (RHEINLAND-WESTFALEN)

I

This region includes part of the lower Rhine plain and of the middle Rhine plateau and it is traversed by the river Rhine from north to south. It lies in the extreme north-west of Germany and borders upon Holland, Belgium and Luxemburg. It is the major industrial region of Germany, accounting for 20 per cent. of its population, 20 per cent. of the people engaged in industry, and 40 per cent. of the installed power from all sources. It has 12 million inhabitants, of whom over 50 per cent. live in towns with over 50,000 inhabitants. It produces four-fifths of the coal of the Reich, 30 per cent. of its brown coal and four-fifths of its pig-iron and steel. This is one of the main modern economic entities of modern Germany. It owes its historic unity to its being a great crossways of routes, centred on Cologne, and its modern unity to its orientation towards the new industrial regions of the Ruhr and the Cologne Bay, which have even further emphasized the inter-dependence of its contiguous highly industrial areas. Most of the area falls into the two Prussian Provinces of Rhineland and Westphalia, and there are indeed many contrasts between these two Provinces arising mainly from their separate administrations. But the unity of the whole is determined by the great development of industry, localized in distinct geographical groupings, by the interdependence of these industrial groupings, by the dominance of the Ruhr in this respect and in respect of the organization and the movements of food supplies, and finally by the historic rôle of Cologne as the capital city.

First, let us glance at the main physical features of the land.

The lower Rhine plain, which is a part of the great Northern Lowland, pushes southwards up the Rhine valley into the plateau as far as Bonn, in a great embayment in the centre of which, on the left bank of the Rhine, is situated Cologne. The plain includes a mixture of heath, moor, and wood, with meadows on its marshy valley floors (notably that of the Rhine plain which is flanked by bluffs), and scattered patches of cultivated land, with hedged fields and isolated farms. The plateau consists of two main features. The rolling surface of the plateau proper and the more rugged hills occasionally rising from it are mainly wooded, with patches of cultivation and clustered villages in their midst. Into this level plateau are cut the deep river valleys. The Rhine, that follows a gorge from Bingen to Bonn, cuts right across the plateau. Its tributaries have a similar character, the Moselle and the Lahn converging on the Rhine in the heart of the rectangular plateau block at Koblenz. These valleys have a dual significance from our point of view. Their lower and more sheltered slopes are clothed with vineyards and they are, and always have been, great avenues of commerce. The Rhine gorge has served from earliest times as a main link, both by the river and by roads alongside it, and to-day by rail, between south Germany and southern Europe and Flanders and the North Sea lands.

Between the plateau and the plain, actually forming the southernmost strip of the latter, there is a narrow belt of country that is strongly contrasted to both these. It is part of the *Börde* zone to which we have drawn attention. It is flat, or gently undulating country, devoted to-day, as for many centuries past, to arable farming. Hedgeless and treeless with large farming villages, its patterns of variegated coloured strips of hedgeless fields stand in marked contrast to the landscapes of plain and plateau on either side of it. This is part of the great belt that traverses central Europe from northern France to the so-called black earth belt of south Russia. It begins around Aachen on the western frontier, and broadens out in the Cologne Bay and then continues east of the Rhine as a narrow strip only a few miles wide between the northern edge of the uplands drained by the Ruhr river and the Emscher river to the north of it, jutting out eastwards through Soest and Paderborn, and pointing like an arrow to the ancient river crossings of the Weser between Kassel and Minden—the latter commanding the famous Westphalian Gate. This strip is called the Hellweg, and its southern edge, the Haarstrang. Beyond the Weser, after a break formed by the uplands that flank it, the belt is continued into central Germany. There are small patches of similar country to the south, both on the plateau and in its valleys. This was the zone of earliest Germanic settlement and for centuries has been its principal and most closely settled farming land and a most important zone of communications.

II

This whole region is by nature a great crossways of over-land routes. The first zone of passage is the open *Börde* zone just noted. From earliest times this has been a zone of east-west movement. The earliest Germanic trackways beyond the frontier of the Roman Empire on the Rhine ran along this zone from near the mouths of the Ruhr and the Emscher east-wards across the Weser crossings to the Elbe at Magdeburg, which was early established by Charles the Great as an outpost of Christianity and trade against the Slav lands to the east of the Elbe. The main seat of the Saxons, when pushed eastwards from their natural fortresses in the lower Weser uplands by Charles the Great, lay beyond the Weser, and their earliest towns appeared on the northern edge of the Harz mountains on the route to Magdeburg. In the Middle Ages this whole zone, from the Rhine to the Elbe, was traversed by a network of east-west high-ways from Flanders in the west to Magdeburg, Leipzig and the newly settled German lands beyond the Elbe. This has been one of the most important highways in European history. It was in connection with it that a number of towns early came into being—Aachen, the capital of the Carolingian empire, that embraced the whole of western and central Europe ; several smaller towns on the routes between it and the Rhine on the northern edge of the Rhine plateau—Jülich and Düren; and, on the Rhine, Cologne, which early displaced the preceding Roman centres at Wesel and Xanten. Beyond the Rhine, along the narrow arrow of open land, lay Duisburg, Essen, Bochum, Dort-mund, Soest and Paderborn. These were on or near the old German highway of the Hellweg. All these were fully-fledged towns by 1200 and the last three among its greatest trade centres.

The second great avenue of settlement and movement is the north-south route of the Rhine. Used as a frontier of the Roman Empire in its lower course, the Rhine was also followed on its west bank by a great highway, that linked together the outposts of that Empire from Basel to Utrecht. This Roman highway never ceased to exist and to be used, and many of its Roman settlements, though their history is obscure during the long dark period of the Germanic invasions, were selected as Christian bishoprics and became also trading centres accessible by road, and by the Rhine, whence came the Flemish merchants from the North Sea shores. The chief of these centres on the lower

Rhine was Cologne. The Rhine gorge remained one of the chief links between north and south Europe both by river and road. The territorial lords owning land on the plateau flanking it fought for vantage points on the river front so as to draw revenue from its prosperous vine-growing villages and from the tolls on the traffic that perforce, by river or road, had to pass through them—a fact which in itself greatly hampered traffic in the later Middle Ages.

There were, of course, many branches from these two main axes. We may note especially the routes up the Moselle from Koblenz to the bishopric and great Roman capital of Trier, and up the Lahn from Koblenz to central Germany upon which grew the historic towns of Wetzlar and Limburgh clustered around their old churches. We may also note the highway that ran from Wesel through Münster, an ancient bishop's seat, to the equally ancient bishops' seats at Osnabrück and Bremen.

The earliest towns in the region all had their origins on these main routes and they included, possibly excepting Düsseldorf, all the chief towns of to-day, as well as many that have remained small and rural, such as Soest and Paderborn and Jülich, in the *Börde* zone and Boppard in the Rhine gorge. Of all these towns by far the most important from the earliest times to this day was Cologne. This city lies on the left bank of the Rhine, at the convergence of these two main axes and situated in the midst of the fertile land of the Cologne Bay.

The Rhine, however, was always a barrier to the expansion of the small states on either side of it until the modern era. Towns, communes and States on opposite sides of the river bank were independent of each other, and there were no permanent bridges until the advent of the railway in the middle of the nineteenth century. Cologne, for example, was essentially a town of the left bank ; Deutz, on the opposite bank, was a small fortress town founded by the bishops of Cologne to command the approaches to the city. Modern industry concentrated in Deutz and Mülheim, but it was not till 1888 and 1914 that these right bank areas were absorbed into the city of Cologne.

III

The development of modern economy and the great growth of population have brought no great shift in this fundamental pattern of pre-industrial settlement, but rather have reinforced it, although considerably whittling down the influence of Cologne through the growth of other of the medieval cities. The first point to note is that the great coalfield of the Ruhr (as well as the small field near Aachen) lie in the *Börde* zone and the great growth of industry and population has been centred in and near the towns that were its pre-industrial capitals. Duisburg-Essen-Bochum-Dortmund, in a west–east series, are the great centres of the " Ruhr ". Here, too, are concentrated, in consequence, the main east–west trunk railways. Essen, whose administrative area lies astride the centre of the whole Ruhr industrial area, taps most of the through railway traffic as well as that of the local traffic around it. It normally dispatches 25 per cent. and receives 15 per cent. of the total goods traffic of the Reichsbahn (the large proportion undoubtedly being due to the heavy traffic in coal) and its issue of passenger tickets normally exceeds that of Cologne.

The improvements of the Rhine as a waterway have made it virtually an arm of the sea, taking barges of 2,500 tons as far as Strasbourg and small sea-going craft to Cologne. Cologne maintains its pre-eminence as a focus of road and rail and owes much to its position on the Rhine. Two main canals run eastwards from the Rhine through the Ruhr industrial area. These are the Rhein-Herne canal, from Duisburg-Ruhrort, and the canalized Lippe, from Wesel, each taking barges of over 1,000 tons to their junction at the eastern end of the Ruhr at Datteln. Thence the canalized Lippe runs to Hamm, and the Dortmund-Ems canal (built 1892-9) branches north passing Münster and following parallel to the Ems to Emden. It takes 750-ton barges. The Mittelland canal branches off at Rheine (40 kilometres north of Münster) and goes due east through Minden and Hanover with a short branch to Osnabrück. The main railway routes—those with the most frequent services and densest traffic—follow the same course as the main overland cross-ways we have noted, namely, Aachen—Cologne—Hanover—Berlin, Frankfurt—Cologne—Utrecht, and Cologne—Essen—Bremen. There is a knotting up of these main routes in the Ruhr together with a dense network of local routes. Here the network lies south of the Rhine-Herne canal and the Cologne Bay. There is also a main line from Düsseldorf through Wuppertal (Elberfeld-Barmen) and the main focus of all these routes lies at the eastern end of the Ruhr at Hamm. The same pattern is emphasized by the direction of the new *Reichsautobahnen*.

A major change in the modern traffic movements is that the great movement of bulk traffic on the Rhine is now centred on Duisburg-Ruhrort, the outlet for the Ruhr which is situated some forty miles downstream from Cologne and is the greatest inland port in Europe. It receives ores, grain and oil upstream from Rotterdam, and dispatches coal both downstream and upstream to southern Germany and Switzerland. Thus, Cologne and Duisburg-Ruhrort and to a lesser extent Düsseldorf are the great key-points of this network of communications in the Rhineland-Westphalian region.

IV

Iron mining and smelting were widespread in the Rhine Plateau from the early Middle Ages onwards. The chief areas lay to the east of the Rhine and there to-day is the chief source of Germany's small iron ore production. The iron-mining districts were the valleys of the Sieg (east of Bonn, known as the Siegerland) and of the Lahn and Dill east of Koblenz, and the plateau of the Sauerland between the Sieg and the Ruhr. Timber, charcoal, and ores were obtained locally, and the forges were located alongside the streams, whose running water was used for power. The Sauerland became the chief centre of mining, smelting and iron-working in the Middle Ages. During and after the eighteenth century as local iron ores were exhausted, the workings began to be shifted northwards towards the Ruhr valley, nearer to the main highways along which ores were imported. Here, too, coal outcropped near the surface and it was mined and carried by cart and donkey to the hammers and forges in the valleys. Steel works grew up in the Ruhr valley and in the Sauerland, using the " puddling process ". It was not till after 1850 that deep shafts could be sunk in the coalfield on the lowland north of the Ruhr valley and its flanking uplands, and by 1860 the pits reached north to the Emscher and by 1900 as far as the Lippe. Since this date, with still deeper shafts, the coal mines have been moved still further north. The iron industry followed in the wake of the coal-mine. The first coke-using furnace was established in 1849. Ores were obtained partly from the coal measures, but in the 'fifties most of the ore came from the Siegerland and the Lahn and Dill valleys. Then ores began to be imported from Spain. The big change came with the development of the Thomas-Gilchrist process in the eighties, which caused a complete reorganization of smelting (from the Bessemer process) so as to utilize the phosphoric ores of the Lorraine *minette* ores. This change resulted in the very rapid growth of the Lorraine field and the closest interchange of iron ore and coke between Lorraine and the Ruhr. Since the last war, Germany has been more dependent on imported ores, and the great bulk of the ores have been imported by the Rhine and the Dortmund-Ems canal. Thus there is a broad contrast between the heavy industrial district on the central belt of the coalfield, and the Sauerland to the south which produces smaller wares that demand small amounts of material and considerable skill and labour. To the south of the Sauerland, the Sieg, Lahn and Dill valleys are still the chief producers of iron ore in Germany. Their ores are sent in part to the Ruhr and coke brought back by the Rhine in return for local smelting. In the Siegerland about half of the ores is smelted on the spot. There is little smelting in the other two valleys owing to transport costs, their ores being smelted near Neuwied on the Rhine or sent by water to the Ruhr.

On the west bank of the Rhine, the iron industry began on the plateau, but has now died out and shifted north to the border of the Eifel plateau where there are two small coalfields (Wurm and Inde) near Aachen. Supplies of calamine accounted for the original location of the brass industry at Stolberg, which now depends on imported zinc and copper. At Aachen iron-working remains, including in particular the manufacture of needles. The textile industries, on the other hand, are especially important on the left bank. They began as a woollen industry in Aachen and the neighbouring towns and as a cottage industry in the Eifel. Raw materials began to be imported in the seventeenth century, flax being replaced by cotton and silk. The change to factory organization was earlier than in the rest of Germany owing to the early exploitation of the coalfield.

V

For several centuries after the break-up of the empire of Charles the Great in the early Middle Ages north-western Germany contained two great dukedoms which were divided by the Rhine—Lower Lorraine and Saxony, which extended south to a north-east–south-west line a few miles south of Bonn. The region fell into several divisions in the late Middle Ages which had stable political frontiers in spite of their apparently kaleidoscopic pattern on the coloured historical maps. The archbishopric of Cologne extended as a strip along the left bank of the Rhine with its centre in Cologne. To the west was the dukedom of Jülich, with its original nucleus and capital in the city of that name, and stretching from the plain on to the Eifel plateau. To the east was the dukedom of Berg, with its capital in Düsseldorf, and covering much of the eastern half of the plateau. The small dukedom of Kleve stretched over the plain on either bank of the lower Rhine. Further to the east lay the extensive territories of the bishops of Münster, and the dukedom of Westphalia on the plateau south of Soest, that belonged to the bishops of Cologne. East of the Ems in the uplands of the Weser there was a group of territories of ancient standing that have always been relatively independent of western relations and more closely tied up with each other and with the sphere of *Niedersachsen* to the east. These were the bishoprics of Paderborn and Osnabrück, and the *Grafschafts* of Lippe and Ravensburg. (The territory of the bishops of Münster also included the lower Emsland). This division of the Weser area with respect to its internal divisions and its relations to adjacent territories has been permanent for over a thousand years and the distinctions are clear in popular feeling and usage. It was not till the formation of the Prussian province of Westphalia, consolidated from many separate political units, that two prongs of Westphalian territory reached out to these Weser lands to include Ravensburg, Minden and Paderborn. In fact, historically, economically and politically this is a zone with a great measure of independence and with relations with the culture spheres both to the west and east of it. To the south in the Moselle valley, lay the bishopric of Trier, to the west lay the United Provinces (later to be known as Holland), Luxemburg and the bishopric of Liége. The temporary phase of French occupation during the Napoleonic Wars brought a reorganization of administrative districts on the French model into departments and *arrondissements*. After the treaty of Vienna in 1815 the whole territory passed to Prussia and there emerged from this historic pattern the two provinces of Rhineland (Rheinland) and Westphalia (Westfalen). Rhineland has a triangular shape with its base in the south and tapering northwards with its hypotenuse on the Rhine. It included roughly the bishopric of Trier, and the dukedoms of Kleve, Jülich and Berg.[1] The boundary between Rhineland and Westphalia is of very ancient origin, the part north of the Ruhr dating from the division of the early medieval dukedoms. Westphalia included roughly the bishopric of Münster and the dukedom of Mark. The boundary between the two provinces ran east of the Rhine and is of very ancient standing, dating from the early Middle Ages, and was a real politico-cultural divide. But the modern economic development, the growth of population and new orientations, have outmoded it, and this old boundary now cuts right through the chief industrial areas of the plateau and through the heart of the Ruhr industrial area that has emerged in the last hundred years.

VI

Rhineland-Westphalia falls into several clearly defined economic units, each characterized by a distinct group of related industries.

(a) *The Heavy Industrial Belt* (Fig. 25) is commonly, though quite inaccurately, referred to as the Ruhr. This is a belt of low and level land on the northern edge of the uplands, known as the Sauerland through which flows the Ruhr from east to west. The river flows in thinly-peopled, wooded, upland country and is used to-day mainly as a source of water and electricity for the industrial area north of it. The industrial area stretches east of Duisburg-Ruhrort, its great river outlet on the Rhine (Ruhrort, meaning the 'place of the Ruhr'). It is a closely settled urban belt stretching from Duisburg to Dortmund, a distance of about 40 miles with a width of about 15 miles. (There is a small outlier of the main coalfield west of the Rhine at Mörs and the extreme eastern end of the coalfield is usually taken as Hamm). To the north is level land under heath and wood and marsh. To the south, there are wooded uplands and deep valleys, which, south of the Ruhr river, are densely settled and industrialized. The belt has about 3¼ million inhabitants and about one-third of its 500 square miles is built-up. It falls into three belts. The southern upland is wooded with patches of cultivation, and very small industrial centres lie along the Ruhr river. The main central belt includes the great urban centres—Duisburg-Hamborn (431,000), Essen (660,000), Bochum (303,000), and Dortmund

---

[1] A province of Jülich-Kleve and Berg was first established in the new Prussian state in 1815. In 1824 this was absorbed with other districts west of the Rhine to form the new province of Rhineland.

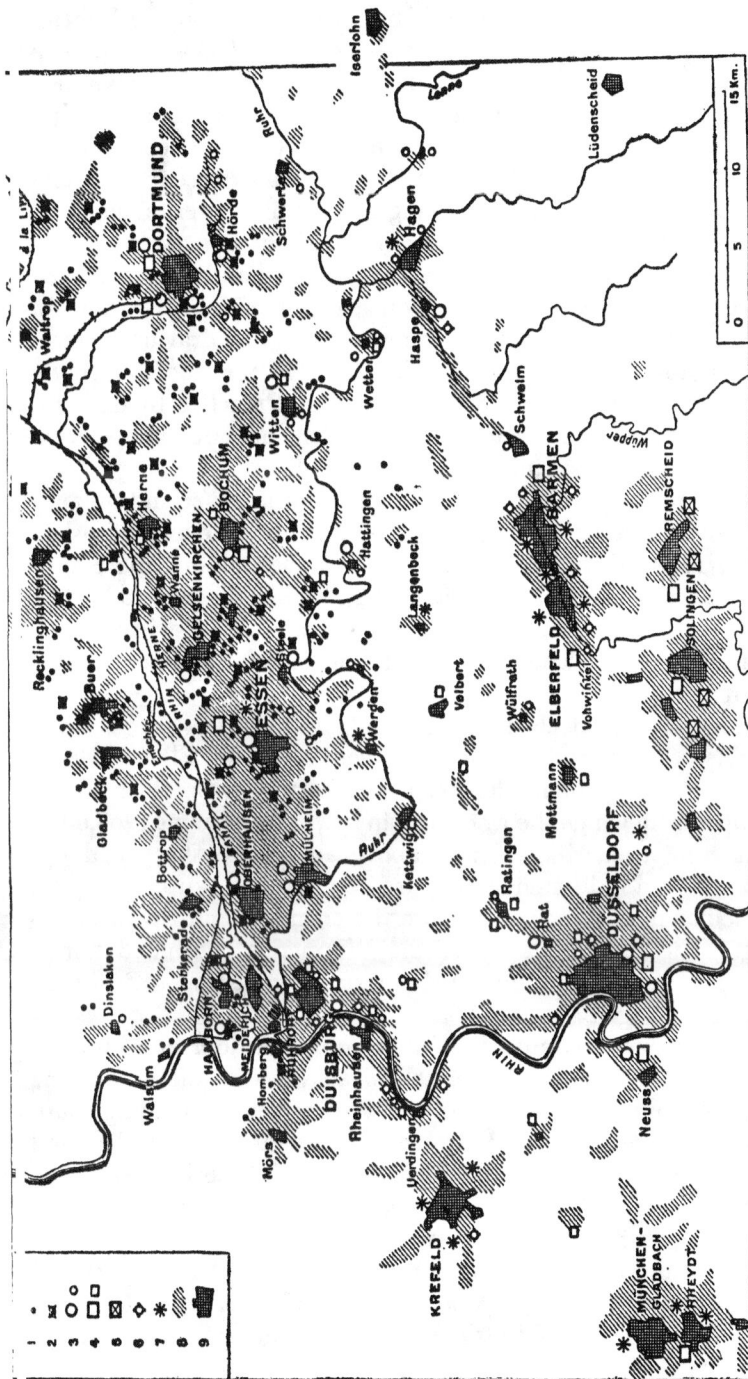

FIG. 25.—The Ruhr and adjacent Industrial Areas.

(After De Martonne, 1930.)

1, coal-mines ; 2, coking plants ; 3, blast furnaces and foundries ; 4, engineering ; 5, ironmongery ; 6, chemicals ; 7, textiles ; 8, built-up areas ; 9, central urban areas.

(537,000), together with Gelsenkirchen (313,000), Mülheim (137,000), and Oberhausen (192,000). The closest built-up area is the western half, west of, and including, Gelsenkirchen and Essen. This belt extends north to the river Emscher and the Rhine-Herne canal. It contains the main coal-mining area, and the heavy industries associated with the coal : iron and steel plants, blast furnaces, rolling mills, coke-batteries and dis-tillation plants and heavy engineering (boilers, locomotives, railroad stock, etc.). All these are predominantly concentrated in the western section, mainly on account of the proximity of Duisburg-Ruhrort and the Rhine whence are drawn the ores from abroad. North of the Emscher is the more recently developed coalfield, here deeply buried and reached by deep pit shafts. Mines and open miners' settlements are interspersed among farm, forest and heath.

(b) *The Wuppertal-Solingen district* lies in the Sauerland uplands south of the Ruhr and is concerned with the production of finished goods, requiring smaller quantities of material but more pro-cessing. These industries are an outgrowth of the old-established ore-mining and charcoal-smelting along the swift-running upland streams. The total population of this scattered area is about three-quarters of a million.

Two industrial clusters are found here.

First, Wuppertal is the combined towns of Elberfeld and Barmen, strung along the deep and narrow floor of the river Wupper from which the whole urban belt takes its name (398,000). Textiles (cotton, silk, carpets, above all haberdashery and up-holstery) and light engineering are dominant in Wuppertal. Of particular importance to-day are the chemical and rayon indus-tries. The narrow valley of the Wupper is continued north-eastwards as a continuous belt of small industrial settlements, ending in Hagen (152,000), another seat of light and old-estab-lished engineering industries in the old dukedom of Mark.

Second, the Solingen-Remscheid area lies on the undulating plateau, immediately south of the Wupper and extending south to the Westerwald. The town settlements are smaller and villages and houses are widely scattered. The principal indus-tries are fine steel wares. Solingen (138,000) and Remscheid (103,000), Lüdenscheid and Iserlohn are the chief seats of iron-mongery and cutlery production in Germany. Velbert (30,000) has virtually a monopoly of the production of keys, and also specializes in household fittings. Much of this industry is carried on in factories, but small workshops and domestic working are very important.

This whole area corresponds with the two stable political units of Berg (West) and Mark (East) for which reason it is often called in Germany the *Bergischmärkische* district. Its dominant commercial centre is Elberfeld.

(c) *The Aachen District* west of the Rhine on the northern border of the Eifel plateau, corresponds in position with the Ruhr. The chief centre, one of the most ancient towns in Europe, is Aachen (165,000), situated on the old west–east highway from Flanders to central Europe and to-day occupying a key position on the German frontier on the great west–east railway axis from Brussels to Cologne. Near to Aachen are two small coalfields, and the town, with the oldest engineering industries in Germany, has varied industries, mainly engineering and textiles. Stolberg is a centre of brass production, depending originally on local ores though now importing zinc and copper. Coal, labour and capital keep the industry where it is. Düren nearby is one of the small towns on the Eifel border that has some modern industry (paper-making).

(d) *The Krefeld-München-Gladbach District* is a textile-manufacturing district. Krefeld (169,000) specializes in silk goods, München–Gladbach (127,000) together with Rheydt (77,000) in cotton goods, with machinery as a secondary industry. There are some heavy chemical and engineering industries at Ürdingen (part of Krefeld) owing to its proximity to the Rhine. Rheydt is a centre of electro-technical industries and textiles and is a part of the same urban complex as M. Gladbach. This urban textile area has a population of about 250,000.

(e) *Cologne-Düsseldorf District.* These two Rhine cities, together with smaller seats of industry on the Rhine—Neuss and Leverkusen—make up a closely related urban group. Together with their satellites, exactly like Duisburg-Ruhrort to the north, they owe their modern industry primarily to the existence of the great artery of thé Rhine and their proximity to the Ruhr, from whence they draw iron and steel for fabrication, and to the textile industrial districts, which they supply with chemicals. Iron and steel smelting, heavy engineering industries, and heavy chemical industries are characteristic of these Rhine-side centres.

Düsseldorf is situated on the right bank of the Rhine, and together with Neuss on the left bank had a population of 600,000 in 1939. It owes its important industries and commercial status to its proximity to the heavy industrial district of the Ruhr, the light industrial district of Wuppertal and Solingen, and to its position on the Rhine, permitting the importing of iron ores. Düsseldorf is a very important seat of heavy and light engineering and is the commercial headquarters for many Ruhr industrial concerns.

Cologne (768,000), the third largest city in Germany, lies on the left bank of the Rhine, though its modern extensions have spread to the right bank where the chief heavy engineering industries are located. Its industries are varied as in all great cities, but the engineering industries are especially important, located on the right bank of the river (Mülheim, Deutz, Kalk). Downstream at Leverkusen is the great seat of the I. G. Farben chemical plant. A new harbour and factory area lies on the north side of Cologne, where the Niehl harbour is projected.

A few miles south-west of Cologne is the great lignite (brown coal) producing area in the Ville district. There has been little concentration of industry in this recently developed area. The brown coal is utilized on the spot in vast briquette and electricity plants, and fuel and electricity are distributed to Cologne and throughout the Rhineland-Westphalia region.

Cologne was the greatest Roman settlement, the greatest medieval archbishopric and city, and is to-day the greatest commercial and cultural centre in north-west Germany. Through the modern growth of industry and commerce, it has grown rapidly, and the built-up area has expanded outwards from the old city and to the new exclusively industrial areas on the right bank. The city has greatly extended its administrative limits, so that it had in 1939 over 750,000 inhabitants living on about a quarter of its vast administrative area (the second in size after Berlin) of nearly 100 square miles. Until the modern era, the prestige and power of the bishops and burghers of Cologne were able to prohibit the growth of any competition within a radius of 30-40 kilometres which is considerably larger than the effective radius of the great medieval cities (normally about 20-25 kilometres.) Even to-day it is surrounded by small towns, the only one of great size, Düsseldorf, owing its growth primarily to the modern development of industry. If the neighbouring places that are economically and culturally a part of Cologne be included in it the population amounts to almost one million. It is the chief commercial and financial centre for the whole of Rhineland-Westphalia.

(*f*) *Münsterland* is the area north of the Ruhr stretching to the Dutch frontier and centred on Münster (144,000). It has relatively little industry and is a country of cultivated land, heath and woods. Both Münsterland and the lower Rhine plain are dairying areas, marketing both fluid milk and fat stock in the urban markets of the Ruhr. Münster, its ancient cultural centre, with its university and cathedral, has attracted industries owing to its favourable situation as a railway centre and its nearness to the Dortmund-Ems canal, which skirts the south-east of the town. Towards the frontier is one of the most ancient seats of domestic handicrafts in Western Europe, like Flanders. To-day, its small towns have cotton and linen industries similar to those of Enschede across the Dutch border.

(*g*) *The Siegerland and Lahn-Dill District (Westerwald)* lies in the eastern half of the Middle Rhine plateau, and includes the Sieg (east of Bonn) and the Lahn and Dill (east of Koblenz). This is an old iron producing and working area and the chief source of Germany's domestic iron ores. The ores are of good grade but costly to work and transport is costly. Ores are smelted on the spot in the Sieg valley, while quantities of coke are imported from the Ruhr in exchange for the dispatch of about half the ore production. But geographically and historically, and in their regional associations, the Lahn and Dill valleys are also closely tied up with Koblenz and the Main-Rhine Region.

(*h*) *The Koblenz Transition District.* In the heart of the rolling Rhine plateau, the deep valleys of the Moselle from the left and the Lahn from the right converge in the Rhine gorge and here in a depression is sited Koblenz, the capital of this area.

East of the Rhine, its sphere includes the Lahn and Dill valleys.

Particularly important on the left bank, in the Eifel plateau, is stone quarrying (volcanic). In addition to the exploitation of the forest (in the past for charcoal and for tannin for the leather industry, now extinct, and at the present for pit-props, etc.). The vine clothes the slopes of the valleys of the Rhine and Moselle —a feature which clearly marks them off from the lower Rhinelands, for the vine is not grown below Bonn. This whole district extends from Siegen in the north-east to Trier in the south-west and has its commercial focus in Koblenz. In effect it has close historical and modern relations with the Rhineland-Westphalian area to the north and the Main-Rhine area to the south.

This great complex of the whole of the Lower Rhinelands, or Rhineland-Westphalia as it is alternatively called in Germany, is the most important industrial area in the Reich, with over two-thirds of its 12 million people dependent on industry and commerce. It has four cities with between 500,000 and a million inhabitants and about a dozen in addition with over 100,000. It accounts for a fifth of the people in the Reich engaged in industry and over two-fifths of the installed power. The Ruhr industrial area produces four-fifths of the coal, pig-iron and steel, and the Cologne area nearly a third of the brown coal. Its commercial unity is due to the economic interdependence of its specialized industrial sectors and to the dominance of its great cities, and above all to the historic and modern economic metropolis of Cologne.

The essential unity of the whole is in many ways divided by the artificial barrier between the two provinces of Westphalia and Rhineland that runs on the right bank of, and parallel to, the Rhine, cutting right through the " Ruhr ". This heavy industrial area, however, and its western extension across the Rhine to the frontier is part of the *Ruhrsiedlungsverband*, the authority legally established in 1921 to care for the common problems of regional planning—zoning, communications, open spaces and water-supply—for the whole " Ruhr " area.

The northern lowlands in particular are brought into the orbit of the food supply for the cities. Milk supplies, for instance, are drawn from a radius of 100 kilometres of Essen, with especially large consignments from the lower Rhine plains and the Münster-land. The same holds good for livestock that are sent to the city slaughterhouses.

Especially important are the economic inter-relations based on the predominance of the Ruhr coalfield and its heavy iron and steel industries, the light iron- and steel-ware industries, the chemicals and textiles. All these industries depend primarily on power—coal and its derivatives (coke, gas, electricity) and lignite (briquettes and electricity).

The proportion of coal to total rail and water traffic is 40 per cent. for the Reich ; it is much larger for Rhineland-Westphalia. From the Ruhr (together with the Aachen field) 82 million tons of coal, briquettes and coke were despatched by rail and barge in 1935. The total was distributed as follows :

Million tons		To
Rail	21·0 . . .	Rhineland-Westphalia.
	7·0 . . .	German seaports.
	16·5 . . .	Other German districts.
	8·5 . . .	Abroad.
Water	6·8 . . .	German ports on the Rhine and Main (for distribution by rail in south Germany).
	1·0 . . .	Alsace and Switzerland.
	16·5 . . .	Netherlands and Belgium.
	3·0 . . .	German seaports.
	1·5 . . .	Other ports of lower Rhine for distribution by rail in north-west Germany.

The trade in brown coal and briquettes from the Cologne field in the Rhineland province amounts to a dispatch of 12·6 million tons in 1935. Most of this was carried over short distances in the provinces of Rhineland and Westphalia, with small quantities of briquettes to Hesse and Lower Saxony. About 2·5 million tons were sent by barge up the Rhine to Baden and the Palatinate for redistribution by rail.

These figures show convincingly that while the Rhine is used for long-distance consignments, the rail is used for regional and general distribution and especially for shorter hauls. If we exclude the consignments to ports and directly abroad, then one-half of the total fuel traffic in the Reich is confined to the two provinces. This may be carried a step further, for the lignite field west of Cologne is primarily a seat of electricity production, and is connected with the electric grid of Westphalia—with its thermal- (notably the Rheinisch-Westfälische Elektrizitätswerk) and hydro-electric plants. The greater part of Westphalia is supplied with electricity by Westphalian concerns (mainly the Vereinigte Elektrizitätswerke Westfalens). But the R.W.E. feeds Rhineland as well as Siegerland and spreads into Westphalia and north of it into the Emsland to south Oldenburg and Diepholz. A wide zone in eastern Westphalia, parallel to the Weser (70 kilometres wide) is fed from plants in Hesse and Hanover.[1]

The limits of the region are wide border zones with distinctive features of their own. This is a feature common to any region. In this case the border areas of special importance are those of Koblenz and Osnabrück-Bielefeld. In the former the Sieg valley is intimately associated economically and historically with the Sauerland and with the Ruhr. The rest of the Koblenz area is a distinct unit with close relations with both Rhineland-Westphalia and Main-Rhine. The Osnabrück-Bielefeld area is a

---

[1] Spethmann, *Ruhrrevier und Raum Westphalen*, pp. 38–42.

clearly defined physical unit bounded by the two belts of V-shaped hills enclosing the small lowland traversed by the Weser. It has had close relations historically with east and west, but in history, as in its present associations, is much more closely linked with Lower Saxony (*Niedersachsen*) to the east. It is a distinct economic province and is centred on its small industrial-cultural capital of Osnabrück. These features are brought out clearly by the map showing the density of road traffic. A dense continuous net extends to lines from Bonn to Arnsberg, Werl and Hamm, and Dorsten and Bocholt in the north. Beyond, to the north and east there is more open rural country with smaller towns as the focal points of radial roads—Münster, which is closely allied with the region, and, further afield, Osnabrück, Bielefeld and Paderborn, which are each geographically separate and very distinct foci bordering on Lower Saxony (*Niedersachsen*).

CHAPTER IV

LOWER SAXONY (NIEDERSACHSEN)

I

Studies of regional associations and schemes for new administrative provinces all agree in the recognition of this unit. Its name, which has no political significance, and first came into use in the sixteenth century, is used generally in regional divisions and recognizes thereby what is, although not clearly defined as to its geographical limits, a real unit of contemporary German life and affairs. The unit is so firmly fixed in general usage since it brings together a heterogeneous collection of interlocking political divisions, of which the most extensive, and, therefore, the nucleus for the whole region, is the Prussian Province of Hanover. The difficulties in modern life brought about by this political pattern prompted a big investigation of the area at the instigation of the *63rd Provinzial Landtag* of Hanover in 1928 with the following directive.

> The *Landesdirektorium* is requested to collect and collate material to indicate what economic and administrative difficulties arise in the economic region of *Niedersachsen* through the existence of *Länder* frontiers. Also to investigate how the consequences of this territorial disunity of the economic region of *Niedersachsen* can be abolished. This work is to be prepared in collaboration with the *Wirtschaftswissenschaftlichen Gesellschaft zum Studiums Niedersachsen* (economic society for the study of Lower Saxony) and presented as a memorandum (*Denkschrift*) to the Provincial *Landtag*.

This investigation, published in 1929 in two large volumes, was prepared by Dr. Kurt Bruning, Lecturer in Geography at the Technical High School of Hanover. This is our main source of reference for detail but there are many other publications on the political, economic and cultural traits and unity of *Niedersachsen*. As an economic unit it is defined for purposes of the investigation by Bruning, as the region of the associated chambers of commerce (*Wirtschaftsbund Niedersachsen-Kassel*), excluding the southern " bulge " of the Kassel area—although this area, divided between Frankfurt and Hanover and not large or strong enough to stand alone in a nation-wide division, has always elected for union with the *Niedersachsen* region (Fig. 26).

79

This definition, it is explicitly stated, does not claim to be based
on any criteria other than economic associations.

This is an area of distinctive character, which has relations
outside of Niedersachsen, but it is pre-eminently a single unit.
It is bounded, according to this investigation, by the Dutch

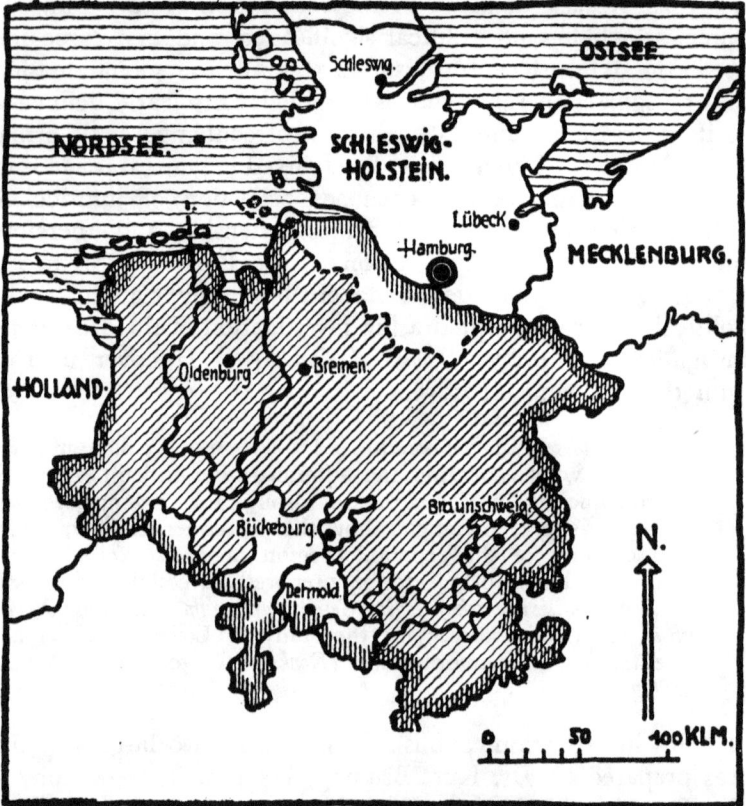

FIG. 26.—*Niedersachsen.*

(After *Niedersachsen im Rahmen der Neugliederung des Reiches*, I Band, 1929.)

Shaded is the area of the *Landesarbeitsamt*, as well as many other trade and
professional organizations. The hatched line defines the area chosen by the *Landes-
direktorium* of the Province of Hanover.

frontier to the west (including the lower Ems land), the Elbe to
the east, a line from north-east to south-west from Salzwedel to
Münden going half-way between Brunswick and Halberstadt to
the south-east and a line north-west to south-east from Rheine
to Münden. The southern end of this diamond-shaped unit
almost reaches Kassel.

Like the author of this work, we also would emphasize that this is a boundary of convenience that follows existing (1929) political boundaries. We choose to regard it as a spring-board for a general discussion of what *Niedersachsen* is.

The name Niedersachsen first appeared in the early sixteenth century, when, in order to introduce some semblance of order and authority in the Empire, the Emperors, overriding the chaotic pattern of feudal territories, established major regions on an Empire-wide basis for purposes of imperial organization—especially for the levying and support of troops. Niedersachsen, embracing the eastern part of the old dukedom of Saxony and the seat of the Saxon Emperors and their people, was so called to distinguish it from Obersachsen, the Wettinian kingdom in the middle Elbe basin, the remnant of which is the modern *Land* of Saxony, with Dresden as its capital. The many maps in the Bruning volumes show the extent of the region for all kinds of *ad hoc* purposes—trade, professional and cultural associations, some important, some of trifling significance—and reveal the consistency with which this area is used. But while its boundaries for these specific purposes are dictated by political lines and therefore appear to be very definite, it will be found in fact that they cut through some districts which are, in all senses, units ; and, in any case, the region merges gradually into neighbours on all sides by reason of its central position. Even in these *ad hoc* maps, however, one notes a frequent and very significant divergence from these political limits. Thus, while the lower Elbe, the boundary of the Province of Hanover, is often the limit, and is taken as such for administrative reasons by the chambers of commerce region, this river cuts right through the Hamburg complex. In fact for this reason many Niedersachsen regions exclude a long strip on the south bank of the lower Elbe, as shown on Fig. 26. On the other hand, the region is sometimes extended beyond the Elbe to include Schleswig-Holstein and Hamburg, while the lower Weser lands (Bremen and Oldenburg) are sometimes excluded. Similarly, the allegiances of the Weser uplands (Osnabrück and Bielefeld) are divided as are those of the Kassel area, and even the northern part of Province Saxony centred on Magdeburg. All these outer areas are in effect a wide " penumbra " to the central heart of Niedersachsen with its capital in Hanover. Ignoring for the moment these questions of zonal limits, the essential feature of the region is that it has its axis, geographically speaking, on the Weser and its flanking uplands and its focus in Hanover, and its nuclear area is the modern province of Hanover.

II

Physically, the region contains four east–west belts of country, which are continued in the regions beyond the Elbe and the Weser. The northern portion of the Central Uplands, drained north by the Weser and the Leine east of it, lies between the Rhine Plateau and the Harz. In history and at present, this country is, from our point of view, especially significant as a region of passage by natural routeways from north to south, through the " corridor " of Hesse, commanded by Kassel and, to a lesser degree, by Göttingen. These uplands merge gradually northwards into a wide zone of rolling, treeless and rich arable country, the *Börde* zone, a continuation of the belt from the Cologne Bay and the Hellweg, from the end of which (after passing through the present industrial towns of the Ruhr) at Paderborn it is separated by the lower Weser uplands around Bielefeld and Osnabrück which here jut north-westwards as a wedge into the lowland. In Niedersachsen this zone extends along the north side of the Harz to the great area of the middle Elbe basin. To the north, making up a good half of the whole area of the region, is a main portion of the Northern Lowland : flat, low-lying land, with moor, heath and meadow, and scattered patches of cultivation on a base of sand and gravel soils (called *Geest*). The marshlands on the northern coast, that extend from the Low Countries in the west to western Denmark in the east, have been drained since the early Middle Ages, while the peat-moors, when denuded of their peat, have been brought under cultivation since the eighteenth century.

The whole region formed in the tenth century the eastern half of the great dukedom of Saxony which extended west almost to the banks of the Rhine, and was bordered by the land of the Frisians in the north coastal marshlands of modern Germany and the Low Countries, including the present province of Holstein beyond the lower Elbe, and the Altmark, centred on Magdeburg. It became the chief habitat of the Saxons after their conquest by Charles the Great, who drove them from their fortress posts in the hills of Westphalia along the Ruhr and Weser. Its first towns appeared in the early Middle Ages along the *Börde* zone and in several isolated centres in the Northern Lowland

(Bremen, Verden, and Lüneburg). The main belt of rural settlement and of town development in the Middle Ages was, however, along the *Börde* zone. This development reached its height in the later Middle Ages. Previously the region was the frontier zone of German settlement.

In the early Middle Ages the region was in fact a borderland ; close German settlement had not even reached the Elbe and there were many islands of Slav settlement between the Elbe and the Weser. The eastward spread of German (Saxon) settlement towards the Elbe began very early and the Elbe for centuries was one of the greatest political and cultural divides in Europe, with its great Germanic and Christian outpost against the Slavs in Magdeburg, situated on the west bank of the Elbe at the end of the main east–west *Börde* route, the continuation of the Hellweg along which so many of the historic cities grew. After about 1150 colonization east of the Elbe began and Niedersachsen occupied thereby a more central position. It should be noted that the land beyond the lower Elbe west of Kiel lay in this original sphere of Saxon culture and settlement.

III

In the later Middle Ages Niedersachsen was crossed by a network of routes. Their main directions were north–south and east–west. The chief east–west routes ran along the *Börde* zone —the zone of most fertile and most closely settled land, and from times immemorial the zone that offered the least difficulty to cross-country movement. The oldest of these ways, existing in early German times in the first millennium A.D., ran as a continuation of the Hellweg eastwards, crossing the Weser at several places, thence passing east along the northern border of the Harz, where some of the earliest Saxon towns developed, to Magdeburg, the great seat of commerce and christianization for the lands it overlooks beyond the Elbe. These *Börde* routes were crossed by north–south routes. The main rivers all flow from south to north, but none of them was ever of great importance for navigation. Far more important were the valleys, that were often followed by the land routes, and the points where they were crossed by east–west routes marked the original sites of many of the towns. In the later Middle Ages with the growth of north–south traffic there emerged a most remarkable concentration of routeways between the Rhine Plateau and the hills of Thuringia and the Harz following the Weser, Fulda and Werra valleys and the Leine. These were all bundled together in the land of Hesse, which for that reason is often referred to by writers as the Hessian Corridor. Here, too, converged routes from across the Rhine Plateau from the Rhine, and from Leipzig and Halle. The two key towns in this ganglion of routes were Kassel and Göttingen. To the north, where the north-south routes opened out to the *Börde* zone, a whole series of important medieval towns appeared as flourishing trading centres. Among these were Halberstadt, Brunswick, Hildesheim, Hanover, Hameln and Minden. These towns grew quickly, but instead of simply expanding from their old centres, two or more entirely separate towns were built adjacent to each other as part of the same settlement, but having independent government and legal existence though cut off from their neighbours at nightfall by the city gates.

The later Middle Ages, however, witnessed territorial disintegration in the area. Though changing in dynastic status, the new territories remained fairly permanent in their extent and acquired real politico-cultural significance. The dukedom of Lüneburg was the nucleus, the predecessor of the kingdom of Hanover. To the east was the old frontier mark of Altmark—the nucleus of Brandenburg and of Prussia of the Hohenzollerns—and the territory of the bishops of Magdeburg. The bishops of Bremen, Hildesheim, Halberstadt, Minden, and Paderborn had their separate territories and, in addition, there were small ducal territories in the Weser hill country—Lippe, Ravensburg and, then further east, the dukedom of Brunswick. In 1815, after the lapse of hundreds of years, the pattern was simplified by the eastward extension of the new Prussian province of Westphalia and the formation of the kingdom of Hanover from the old dukedom of Lüneburg, while the Elbe territories became a part of the new Prussian province of Saxony. To-day, the great part of the region falls into the Prussian province of Hanover together with the political territories embedded in it. These are the *Land* of Oldenburg, the Hansa City of Bremen, the *Länder* of Lippe and Schaumburg-Lippe, and Brunswick, broken up into several isolated and irregularly-shaped parts.

The importance of Niedersachsen as a crossways is no less apparent in the development of modern commerce by rail, road and water. The Weser is the only large river and this flows from south to north through its centre. But it never has been of great importance as a navigable highway like the Rhine or the Elbe, although it is being made accessible to Münden at the confluence of the Fulda and Werra and the latter is being improved and regularized. These north-south rivers are of chief importance as affording lowland routeways for road and rail. There is now completed the Mittelland canal that links the Rhine and Elbe and traverses the northern edge of the populous foreland zone. This great waterway, taking barges of over 1,000 tons, has already made possible the localization of heavy industries around Hanover and the development of the Göring iron and steel plant near the iron ores of Salzgitter. Similarly there is a high density of rail and roads in the *Börde* zone, south of the line of the Mittelland canal, that borders the northern heath and moorlands. Especially important are the great trunk railways from Cologne and the Ruhr to Berlin, and the north-south routes from Hamburg and Bremen to Frankfurt through the important railroad centre of Kassel. The same focusing of trunk routes is evident in the *Reichsautobahnen*, one route running east-west linking Magdeburg-Hanover and the Ruhr with the intervening cities, and a second running north-south from Hamburg to Frankfurt, the crossways being Hanover, from which another route was planned before the war to run north-west, skirting Bremen to Emden. The other main focal points which will stand out in the completed plan of autobahns are Magdeburg, Brunswick and Kassel. Hanover, with 472,000 inhabitants, is the geographical centre of the region, the capital of the old kingdom of Hanover and of the Prussian province, and its traditional regional economic and cultural metropolis.

IV

Niedersachsen is also considered to be a unit from the cultural point of view, albeit it is vaguely geographically defined. Indeed, it is in this sense that the name has become popular in recent years. This conception is based primarily on the past cultural history and its expression in the culture forms and social traits of to-day. In origin, the Saxon people spread westwards beyond the Weser, and at the time of Charles the Great's conquests, their principal refuges were in the tangled hills and valleys of the Sauerland and the Weser uplands. Driven eastwards beyond the Weser, this territory, as far as the Elbe, became their homeland. The western sector, grouped around Münster and the Hellweg towns

(Soest and Paderborn and Dortmund) was more deeply impregnated by Frankish culture and the Roman Church, while east
of the Weser the folk retained a strong pagan tradition and went
over to the Protestant Church with the Reformation. The same
basic dialect—*Niederdeutsch* or Low German—is spoken throughout. To-day, the southern boundary of Low German runs from
Magdeburg south of west through the confluence of the Werra
and Fulda. The western boundary runs east of and parallel to
the Rhine—the boundary between the present provinces of
Westphalia and Rhineland. The contrasts between Westphalia
and Lower Saxony have already been noted in their political
aspects—a group of territories in the west dominated by the
Roman Catholic bishoprics of Soest, Paderborn and, above all,
Münster, and the dominance east of the Weser of the Hanover
province and its long predecessors, which became Protestant.
Here, too, east of the Weser, after the Frankish conquests in the
eighth century, the Saxon folk finally settled, with a mode of
settlement and a legal and cultural life, based on a pagan tradition, very distinct from that of the Rhinelands. In the west, the
church-village is characteristic of the country settlements and
the open market town as in England and northern France and the
Low Countries, whereas castles and walled towns are relatively
few—the distinctive trait being the moated country mansion and
the lavish town mansion of the landed gentry built during the
seventeenth and eighteenth centuries. In Niedersachsen, on
the other hand, half of the land in the north is taken up by the
expanses of heath and moor with small villages and market towns.
But in the *Börde* and the uplands to the south along the great
routeways the oldest towns grew around fortified cathedrals and
secular burghs or fortresses and feudal castles—as evidenced by
the frequency of the suffix *burgh* in town place-names. Many
market settlements were founded in the twelfth century and
almost all of them became walled towns. It is here that one
finds in particular the foundation of twin towns, as at Brunswick, evidencing the great prosperity and rapid growth of these
towns in the Middle Ages.

Niedersachsen is not only the birthplace of the pagan culture
of the Saxons, with all its fundamental divergences from Roman
Christian civilization, whose roots nurture modern Prussianism
and the Nazi movement. The people also, as anthropologists
agree, have dominantly Nordic racial traits. It is the home of
the Saxon tribes, later emerging as the Saxon dukedom which

had its own code of laws with a rich individual folklore and tradition. Here, too, distinct culture forms emerged, though it is not possible to define their geographical limits except vaguely. One of the most distinctive features, apart from speech (*Niederdeutsch*), is the traditional build of the farmstead—the so-called Lower Saxon farmstead—a great half-timbered building in which living quarters, barns and stalls and stables are all under one roof, with a traditional style of building and design. Similarly architectural styles and designs appear in the towns, marking them off as a group from the neighbouring areas.

This culture area of Niedersachsen, with its nucleus in the lands midway between the Weser and the Elbe, and changing gradually southwards in the Central Uplands of Hesse, also merges gradually to the east and the west. To the east, the original culture sphere of the Saxons did not reach to the Elbe and it will be remembered that Magdeburg for long was an outpost, and the Altmark, the nucleus of Brandenburg, lay on the west side of the Elbe. In fact, this was the first zone of colonization by the Saxon people. Schleswig and Holstein, east to Kiel, have the same culture forms and dialects—Saxon, and Frisian on the north coast—as west of the Elbe. In the later Middle Ages (after 1200) with the spread of German settlement east of the Elbe the settlement of the Baltic provinces and Brandenburg was effected by Saxon people, who carried thither their dialects, customs and house forms, and systems of village settlement, all of which were gradually modified from the parent type in the new physical and social environment. All this may appear to be merely academic. Such, however, is not the case, for these traditional regional differences are very strong in Germany, where the rural way of life has not in any way been swamped by the growth of urbanism as in Britain. Moreover, the spread of the Saxon peoples has been such that their area is broadly identical with that of modern Prussia and it is upon the pagan Wagnerian tradition that the Prussian and Nazi ways of life, as distinct from the Western Christian way of life, are largely based.

V

Let us now turn to a brief discussion of the present economic character and associations of this region of Niedersachsen. Mineral resources are small and scattered and have, in consequence, not given rise to any great urban agglomerations such as are found to the east and west of it in the Ruhr and in the middle Elbe basin. Coal is mined in the lower Weser hills near Osnabrück and Ibbenbüren, and there is a small field in the Deister district near Hanover. Iron ores are mined at Peine, east of Hanover, and Salzgitter, 10 miles south-west of Brunswick. Oil is obtained near Celle on the northern lowland and salt at various points east of Hanover, especially around Hildesheim. These resources are scattered and scanty and cannot support heavy industries. The main industrial districts are in and around Brunswick and Hanover, and form a continuation geographically of the industrial district of Central Germany around the northern edge of the Harz south of Magdeburg. Beet sugar, brown coal and salt industries figure in both districts, but in the former none is dominant and it is better characterized as a zone of mixed industries. Industry is also mainly clustered around the towns, especially Hanover and Brunswick. Here alone is to be found over a half of Germany's rubber industry. The industrial development of these two districts has been greatly stimulated by the opening of the Mittelland canal, which runs from east to west a few miles to the north of these towns. Elsewhere, industry is of little importance except for Salzgitter where the Hermann Göring works are situated. A special industry with the chief seat in Germany around Brunswick, is the manufacture of preserves, which has developed since the 'sixties, in association with the cultivation of asparagus. But Brunswick is of chief importance to-day for its light engineering industries.

The Weser hill country in the west forms a separate and distinct industrial complex. Wood and sand favoured in the past the early development of a glass industry. The oldest centre was in the Solling district, dating from the eighteenth century, which to-day, depending on its skilled labour supply, produces high grade goods, including half of the world's production of spectacle lenses. West of the Weser, the linen industry was of very ancient origin. The old-established cottage industry as elsewhere in Germany, was badly hit in the early nineteenth century by the competition of cheap English factory wares, and instead of being adapted to the new conditions (the rulers of Lippe actually forbade the import of textile machinery in the early days), it virtually died out, and its place was taken by new industries. In the north—the Minden district—cigar-making appeared (as in the Eichsfeld) and is to-day the dominant industry. In the south—the *Land* of Lippe—wood-working grew, together with cigar-making ; the main branch is the making of furniture. The Ravensburg district, centred on Bielefeld, is an old linen-making district, too, but it has developed new and distinct industries. Bielefeld is still a main seat of the linen industry, but from it has grown a variety of new and related industries—related in the sense of continuing the same kind of labour and producing goods requiring the same sort of skill and work—such as the making of sewing machines and bicycles.

Hanover owed the beginnings of its modern industrial development to the proximity of the Deister coalfield. But its real industrial growth did not commence till the 'sixties with the advent of the rubber industry for which it is Germany's chief centre of production. In the next decades, the textile and automobile industries were added and for both of these it is to-day an outstanding centre.

Thus, Niedersachsen has its nucleus in the *Börde* zone, in the drainage area of the middle Weser and the Leine rivers, between the Weser hills and the Harz. This is a closely settled and highly productive agricultural area, and has many historic cities, though most are to-day small and retain much of their medieval character. From the commercial point of view it is pre-eminently a region of transit. But its regional life and its politico-cultural development reveal it as a distinct entity, with its capital in Hanover, which is now able to forge ahead as a seat of both light and heavy industries, thanks to its traditional skilled industries, and its position mid-way between the Ruhr and Berlin, and between Hamburg and Frankfurt, while the recent completion of the Mittelland canal has given to the Hanover and Brunswick districts a new lease of industrial life. Finally, this was the original habitat of the Saxon peoples and of the seats of the Saxon Emperors of the Holy German Empire, and the home of the pagan traditions of the German Saxons, in which are rooted Prussianism and its successor, Nazism. The cult of paganism and the Nordic myth, nurtured by the Nazis, has added to the disruption between the Latin and Western Christian traditions of Germanic civilization.

Around this nucleus there are wide areas with a great measure of independence in their historical and economic development and associations. These are the Osnabrück-Bielefeld area, the Kassel area, and the Magdeburg area. Finally, in the thinly peopled expanses of the Northern Lowland, amidst the reclaimed marshes of the North Sea coast are the great ports of Hamburg and Bremen, both historically and economically separate units, which, it is generally conceded, should be regarded as separate from Niedersachsen, and demand recognition as units in a new Reich. The assessment of conditions of historical development and the wishes of present economic interests (as expressed through the district chambers of commerce) associate the Kassel region with Niedersachsen rather than with Main-Rhine, although it lies in the Prussian Province of Hessen-Nassau. The same holds good for the Osnabrück-Bielefeld districts, which, though partly brought into the political orbit of the west through the expansion of Westphalia in 1815, are, in fact, politically, historically, and economically, far more closely allied with Niedersachsen together with the other lands of the Weser basin than with Westphalia.

CHAPTER V

THE LOWER ELBE AND WESER : HAMBURG AND BREMEN

I

The cities of Hamburg and Bremen, situated on the estuaries of the Elbe and Weser respectively, are essentially independent, specialized economic communities, which have grown as great ports serving extensive hinterlands, rather than as seats of regional integration. Though situated on the northern border of Niedersachsen and closely related to it in their cultural associations, the life and interests of these cities are tied up with their ports and their world-wide connections. This has always been so, and for centuries, since the Middle Ages when they were Hanseatic cities, they have been independent states, and it is generally agreed that this status should be retained in a new arrangement of political units in the Reich. In the case of Hamburg, such reorganization has become a vital need for the normal functioning of the life and organization of the agglomeration as a whole, of which Hamburg is only a part. Hamburg in particular illustrates well the fact that the organization of a port, the spread of settlement from its overcrowded core, and the need for adequate transport services from work-place to home and to remoter suburban districts demand the administrative unity of the whole complex, unhampered by the restrictions imposed by other administrative units close around it, which inevitably have impeded far-sighted planning in the great period of growth in the last seventy years.

These two cities, like twins in their historical development and modern economic functions, have also, broadly speaking, the same physical setting. The old city centres lie at the head of broad estuaries that are bordered almost throughout by strips of flat marshland, reclaimed through centuries, dyked, drained and cultivated. These are bordered by slightly higher sandy heathland, known as *geest*, with series of small towns and villages situated at the edge of the marsh and the heath. The latter sometimes reaches the river front as high bluffs, favouring the siting of settlements. This is notably the case at Vegesack and Blumenthal below Bremen. There are, however, big differences between the two cities and their environs. The Weser does not offer the same natural facilities for navigation as the Elbe. Bremen is far upstream and it has not been possible to maintain the estuary in such a condition as to permit the largest modern vessels to reach Bremen itself. Hamburg can be reached without difficulty by the greatest vessels without locks. The Elbe offers a vast hinterland easily accessible by large barges ; on the main river alone—to say nothing of its contact with Berlin—barges of 850 tons burthen can reach 970 kilometres upstream to Aussig in Czechoslovakia, and it is not surprising that most of Hamburg's bulk cargo is trans-shipped direct from boat to barge. The Weser, on the other hand, has serious difficulties to navigation : shallowness and irregularity of flow from season to season. It can take barges of only 350 tons to Kassel, and the upper basin is at present virtually beyond the reach of the barge. The main connection of the lower Weser is with the Mittelland canal, but the extent of Bremen's field of competition is limited by the waterways serving Hamburg and Emden. Railway traffic accounts for 85 per cent. of the goods coming to Bremen from the interior as compared with only 40 per cent. for Hamburg. In view of the differences in the two estuaries, while port facilities on the Elbe have been centralized at Hamburg, they have been naturally decentralized on the Weser below Bremen, the chief centre. Finally, as a result of these differences, while Hamburg and its contiguous urban areas houses quite one and a half million people, Bremen itself houses under 350,000, and even with the smaller ports downstream, under 500,000 people.

II

Hamburg grew on the north bank of the Elbe. Its rise as a great port dates from the Renaissance period with the growth of transoceanic commerce and the decline of the Hanseatic League, with its capital in Lübeck, 45 miles away on the Baltic side of the peninsula. In 1567 the first German Exchange was opened here and soon after the Merchant Adventurers shifted their headquarters from Antwerp. Already by 1800 it had more than 100,000 inhabitants and reached 260,000 in 1866. In 1933 the city of Hamburg alone had over a million inhabitants. But this figure does not include the built-up areas contiguous with Hamburg but outside its administrative limits. Altona, on its west side, with fishing, engineering and food industries, had 242,000 inhabitants. Altona was, in origin, a Holstein founda-

tion, peopled by Dutch colonists.   Beyond it downstream extends
an open and extensive residential district, Blankanese, on higher
geest land overlooking the river   To the north-east there is Wandsbek, with its confectionery industries, with 50,000 inhabitants.
But even more significant is the extension of the great modern
port, to the south side of the river.   Here, on the sea-level marshes,
the cutting of the new docks began in the 'sixties, the old harbour
on the north side adjacent to the old town being far too congested
and offering no space for expansion.   Here has grown the vast
modern harbour with its wharves, warehouses, shipbuilding yards
and factories ; and there are plans for the further extension of
the harbour downstream.   Behind this great port is the industrial
town of Harburg-Wilhelmsburg, with 113,000 inhabitants in
1933, processing the raw materials brought in through the port
—rubber, vegetable oils, chemicals, etc.   Harburg-Wilhelmsburg
was established as a rival port to Hamburg by the rulers of
Brunswick-Lüneburg, then passed to the kingdom of Hanover
and finally to Prussia.   Even with its excellent facilities for
navigation, Hamburg has its outport at Cuxhaven at the southern
tip of the Elbe estuary.   In all this great urban complex there
are over one and a half million inhabitants (1,682,000 in 1939),
the great bulk of them living on the north side of the river,
clustered around the old town and the modern business district
between the Alster lake and the old harbour, while the main
areas of work—port and factories—are situated on the south
side.   In consequence, there is a tremendous congestion of traffic
and serious traffic difficulties.   In 1925 some 37,000 workers
lived in the central business district, but 125,000 found their
occupations there.   In the early 'thirties the port and its related
industries occupied 155,000 persons, so that altogether about
225,000 persons (excluding their dependants) found employment
in the city or port, but less than a fifth of them lived in these
districts.   This raised problems of housing, which have been
made more difficult by the fact that the administrative area of
Hamburg itself was too small to cope with the houses needed, and
this partly explains the predominance of the flat in modern Hamburg.   The traffic problem, both to the central business district,
and, more serious, across the river by ferry, by rail and by tunnel,
is very similar to that of Merseyside, although in the latter far
more of the port workers live behind their port and factory areas.
Then, again, there are the problems of the port—the need for
extensions, for common regulations for the whole port area, and

the rest. Hamburg and its neighbours have their main interest in the river, but they also need elbow-room for expansion radially outwards, both to the north and south of the river.

The problem of the territorial reorganization of the Greater Hamburg complex has long been a source of serious concern, and it is small wonder that many schemes have been put forward since the question of a *Neugliederung* of the Reich came forward after the 1914–18 war. Not only were the four main towns of the group (Hamburg, Altona, Harburg-Wilhelmsburg, Wandsbek) administratively independent of each other, but they were surrounded by the administrative districts, eight in number, of two provinces of Prussia, Schleswig-Holstein and Hanover. Almost the whole of the south side of the river was Prussian territory (Hanover). The earlier schemes for a division of the whole of the Reich included Schleswig-Holstein and Hamburg with Niedersachsen. But economic considerations indicate the essential separateness of Hamburg. The boundary of Niedersachsen is often taken along the Elbe, thus in fact dividing the whole complex through its main artery, an absurd arrangement. But for many purposes Niedersachsen excludes a strip along the south bank of the lower Elbe down to the sea, recognizing thereby the unity of this strip with the Hamburg complex. The minimum area demanded by a new region on the lower Elbe is one comparable with the voluntary association for purposes of regional planning, a radius of 30 kilometres from the centre of Hamburg. It may also be argued that through the concern of the port with the whole of the estuary, the latter should be included in its region. This would bring in a strip some 20 or 30 kilometres wide, but would incorporate large areas of thinly peopled rural land foreign to the urban complex and its activities and outlook. Again, alternative proposals have been put forward, each stressing some particular point of view, e.g. for the inclusion of Lübeck with the Lower Elbe, forming a strip across the neck of the peninsula, separating Schleswig-Holstein from Mecklenburg ; or, again, the inclusion of Hamburg with Schleswig-Holstein and Lübeck. These various proposals need not concern us here. The main fact is that there should be a minimum unit area embracing the whole of the port and urban complex of the lower Elbe with adequate space around, to north and south of the river, for future expansion. A partial solution to this problem was effected in 1937 after many years of dispute—one of the advantages of a totalitarian government. The four towns on the lower

Elbe were then combined to form the one unit of Greater Hamburg. After the somewhat fantastic schemes for the extension of Hamburg put forward from 1918 to 1922, a Hamburg-Prussia arrangement established a common port authority (*Hafengemeinschaft*)—for it will be remembered that most of the port lies on Prussian soil—and a regional planning committee was formed, without, however, any change of political boundaries. The decree of 26th January, 1937, created the new *Hansastadt* Hamburg, including Altona, Harburg, Wilhelmsburg, and a strip of land on the south bank of the Elbe to facilitate the expansion of the harbour downstream, and districts on the north and north-east (including Wandsbek) to bring in the existing built-up areas and allow for their future extension. Several outlying districts have been absorbed into the Prussian *Landkreise* (see Fig. 27).

III

The Lower Weser Region is the term that has been given to the whole of the lower Weser from a little way above Bremen itself to the mouth of the river at Bremerhaven and Wesermünde. Bremen, like Hamburg, was an important member of the Hanseatic League. It was also the seat of a very ancient, bishopric, which was the initial cause of its development as a town. But with the growth of transatlantic trade and the increased size of ships, Bremen already had difficulties with the navigation of the Weser estuary, and in 1618 Vegesack was founded as an outport. Soon after the foundation of Vegesack, ships had to use small ports farther downstream—Elsfleth and Brake—and goods were transferred to Bremen by smaller vessels. For a long period Bremen stagnated, but after 1800 the river was deepened and straightened. The change came after the Napoleonic Wars. In 1827 Bremen purchased from the king of Hanover a strip of land at the mouth of the Weser where it is joined by the Geeste river, and founded there an outport, Bremerhaven. This was able to accommodate the largest vessels afloat and enabled Bremen to become one of the greatest European ports in the nineteenth century, and especially to concern itself with the trade with the United States. Then came the need for improving the river upstream to Bremen itself. This was undertaken in the 'eighties, and the new harbour was opened in stages below the town on the right bank of the river. The great steamship line of Hapag was established in 1847 with its headquarters in Ham-

Legend:

■ Administrative Area of Hamburg

▨ Prussian Territory added to Hamburg

⦙ Hamburg Territory added to Prussia

KREIS PINNEBERG

Winzeldorf
Garstedt
Bönningstedt
Ellerbek
Egenbüttel
Rellingen
Appen
Pinneberg
Lokstedt
Halstenbek
Holm
Schenefeld
Wedel
STADTGEBIET ALTONA
KREIS
Borstel
Königreich
Hove
Finkenwerder
Altenwerder
STA HA
ELBE
Neuenfelde
Francop
Moorburg
Moorende
zu
Rübke
Fischbeck
Neugraben
WILHELMBURG
Neuwerk
STADE
Walmstorf
Cuxhaven
estorf
Marmstorf
Aberstorf
Ehestorf
Vahrendorf
Bechterof
Nordsee
Amt Ritzebüttel
Netzendorf
Levensen
Tötendorf
Altenwalde
Altenbruch
KRE
Spiekeroog Neufeld
Nordholz
Lüdingworth
HA

FIG. 27.—Greater Hamburg as defined

Bargfeld-Stegen
Jersbek
K R E I - S
S T O R M A R N
Harks-heide
Tang-stedt
Wulks-felde
Zu-Duvenstedt
Kl.-Hansdorf
Todendorf
Glas-hütte
Duven-stedt
Wohl-dorf-Ohl-stedt
Hois-büttel
Bünning-stedt
Ober
Lemsahl-Melling-stedt
Berg-stedt
Ahrensburg
Groß Hansdorf
Hois-dorf
Poppen-büttel
Volks-dorf
Hum-mels-büttel
Sasel
Ahrens-felde
Mellings-büttel
Siek
Bramfeld
Farmsen
Rahlstedt
Stapel-feld
Braak
Steils-hoop
STADTGEB.
WANDSBEK
Stellau
K R E I S
Barsbüttel
Willing-husen
Billstedt
Ost-Steinbek
Glinde
LAUEN-BURG
HAMBURG
DTGEB. RBURG
Havig-horst
Lohbrügge
Reinbek
Wohl-torf
Wen-torf
Marsch-und Vierlande
Börn-sen
Esche-burg
Hohen-horn
Worth
Neuland
Bullen-hausen
Ham-warde
Rönne-burg
Meckel-feld
Over
Düne-berg
Geest-hacht
Grunhof-Tesper-hude
Ober-mar-schacht
Flee-tedt
Hörsten
Vossenweide
Fliegen-berg
Hoopte
Stöckte
Stelle
R B U R G

by Nazi decree on January 26, 1937.

burg. In 1857 the second great German shipping company, the Norddeutscher Lloyd, was established with its headquarters in Bremen and identified particularly with the trade with the United States. Thus, in contrast to Hamburg, where from the beginning port facilities have been centralized and there has been no cause to shift them downstream, the lower Weser has been so unfavourable to navigation that its trade has been decentralized, for varying periods and functions, among smaller ports below Bremen. In our day, the chief facilities have become centred in Bremen and Bremerhaven. Thus, there is the original outport of Vegesack, as well as Blumenthal and Elsfleth (30 kilometres below Bremen), and Brake and Nordenham (10 kilometres above Bremerhaven). Wesermünde has grown from the fusion of several parishes beginning with Geestemünde on the Weser and Lehe near Bremerhaven, Geestemünde being established by the king of Hanover in 1857 as a competitor to Bremerhaven. It is to-day the greatest fishing port in Germany, with a population of 75,000. Politically, it belongs to Prussia, though Bremerhaven, that is part of the same urban complex, belongs to Bremen.

Bremen's development as a port has been centred on the American trade. In the nineteenth century it handled the great emigrant traffic to the States. Unlike Hamburg, its traffic is in smaller bulk goods—cotton, wool, grain, and tobacco—since it lacks the port facilities and the hinterland connections of Hamburg. Thus, while Hamburg handles over a half of the foreign tonnage of Germany's overseas trade, Bremen handles only 12 per cent. Both the port and the industries are thus relatively small as compared with Hamburg. Bremerhaven, taking the largest vessels, handles about a fifth of the total trade. The chief plants are in the Bremen port (*Deschimag*), at Vegesack (*Vulcan*), Wesermünde and Einswarden, and there are furnaces at Bremen and Nordenham. Textiles are manufactured at Blumenthal, Bremen, Nordenham and Hemelingen, while Delmenhorst, a satellite to the west of Bremen, about 20 kilometres distant, is a textile centre.

Bremen (342,000) itself lies on slightly raised ground running north-west-south-east on the right bank of the Weser, and its present built-up area is continued to the north by Vegesack (4,000) and Blumenthal (14,000), and to the south by Hemelingen (12,000), the centre that handles the great bulk of its incoming railway traffic. The population of the whole Lower Weser belt from Bremen down to Bremerhaven-Wesermünde is about 750,000.

The latter is a separate built-up focus, with over 100,000 persons (Bremerhaven, 25,000, and Wesermünde, 75,000). While the adjacent built-up area of Bremen has about 35,000 people, it is surrounded by thinly peopled *geest* land, and within 50 miles there are only five places with 10,000 to 100,000 inhabitants. A radius of 10 kilometres includes about 350,000 people, and 25 kilometres about 500,000. Thus, Bremen is about one-third the size of the Hamburg complex.

The lower Weser, together with Delmenhorst, is a centre of overseas trade, shipping companies, passenger traffic, industry and fisheries. Bremen is the biggest cotton market in Europe, the second German port, the seat of one of the two great German shipping companies, and of the greatest shipbuilding firm, while Bremerhaven is the greatest passenger port in Europe for American trade, and Wesermünde the biggest fishing port. Blumenthal and Delmenhorst are among the chief centres of the woollen textile industry in Germany.

The political division of the lower Weser and its banks has been a deterrent to the development of the lower Weser navigation. Around the town and *Land* of Bremen are the territories of Oldenburg and Prussia with an outlier of Brunswick to the south of Hemelingen. The territory of Oldenburg actually overlaps the lower Weser north of Elsfleth. Locally, there is need for the increase of the administrative area of Vegesack and its neighbours and of Bremerhaven-Wesermünde to allow them elbow-room for expansion, and the certain need for the unified control of the whole of the lower Weser waterway.

There remains the possibility of the formation of a new administrative unit together with Oldenburg and the lower Ems. Oldenburg is a small port with considerable industry. Historically there is much in common between these districts, for the counties of Friesland, Jever, Oldenburg, and the Free City of Bremen have always had much in common and are more closely connected to one another than to the lands south of them. Oldenburg and Bremen together form one of the Nazi Regional Planning districts and approximately the same area forms their Party Gau district.

CHAPTER VI

SOUTHERN GERMANY : RHINE-MAIN, SOUTH-WEST, BAVARIA

Southern Germany may be defined in broad terms as the section south of the Rhine Plateau, the Vogelsberg and the Thuringian highlands, including the political units of Baden, Wurtemberg, Bavaria, Rhenish Palatinate, Saar and Hesse-Nassau. It also has close relations, historically, culturally and economically, with Alsace and Lorraine on the west of the Rhine. Politically and economically, this whole area falls into several distinct cultural entities, that, especially in the Rhinelands, were obscured by political disintegration until the formation of the existing political units at the beginning of the nineteenth century. It lacks coal and iron but its industrial development in the nineteenth century was favoured by the support of the small independent States within their own restricted frontiers. Agriculturally also it falls into several distinct regions. These facts of regional integration are further emphasized by the welding of their interests and associations in the cities. These are all historic cities, that have always centralized and organized, in large measure, the cultural, political and economic life of the land without any shifts of population or of city centres. This applies in particular to Frankfurt and Mainz that for centuries have extended their influence across the medieval political divisions, thus giving unity to the whole region around them. Thus, we may recognize a broad similarity of economic function and development in much of southern Germany with several distinct regions based upon separate regional associations. These are the South-west, Rhine-Main and Bavaria. Alsace and Lorraine west of the Rhine form separate regions with close international relations with the Romance and Germanic spheres, but are intimately tied up with the whole question of the navigation of the Rhine. Alsace, in particular, has close regional associations with south-western Germany.

Let us deal first with the general characteristics of southern Germany as a whole and then with the economic and social structure, and the essential unifying characteristics of each of its major units, the Rhine-Main region, the South-west, and Bavaria.

I

Southern Germany is made up of zones of different types of country, radiating fanwise from the Belfort Gap between the Vosges and the Jura in the extreme south-west corner of the Reich beyond Basel. The upper Rhine plain, with an average width of about 30 miles, stretches from Basel northwards for 170 miles to Bingen at the beginning of the Rhine gorge. This is one of the most fertile and closely settled lands in Europe. It is sheltered by belts of wooded uplands, the Vosges and the Hardt to the west, the Black Forest, Odenwald and Spessart to the east. East of the latter is the basin of the rivers Main and Neckar, a confused country of treeless arable land on level fertile plateaus, steep hill and valley slopes, with orchards and vineyards and villages at their feet, and woods on steeper slopes and poorer soils. This basin is encircled by wooded uplands— the so-called Franconian and Swabian Jura. Beyond the former is the wide lowland of the Upper Palatinate, which is bounded to the east by the uplands of the Bohemian Forest. South of the Swabian Jura upland is the Danube valley. The extensive plateau of southern Bavaria lies south of the Danube and reaches the foot of the Alps—or, rather, the range of uplands known as the Prealps that herald the approach to the high Central Alps. This plateau tapers to the west near Basel and to the east in the Danube gorge at Passau before the valley opens out to Vienna. It has a smooth surface with many shallow valleys and a mixture of open fertile farm land, lakes, coniferous forest and marsh.

The frontier of the Roman Empire followed, in general, the Rhine and the Danube, but here in south-western Germany it crossed the country between them as a line of fortifications from Regensburg to near Frankfurt, so as to enclose the whole of the Neckar basin. The Germanic settlers in the first millennium, as in the north, sought out the open forest-free areas, and the main areas of settlement were in the Rhine plain, the Neckar basin and the Bavarian plateau. Here were also situated the chief Roman centres, which in turn became the sites of the first bishoprics and the first medieval towns. From the Rhineland the frontier of close German rural settlement was carried eastwards, from Mainz and Frankfurt up the Main, where the bishoprics of Würzburg and Bamberg were founded, and down the Danube, where a series of towns was established in succession, ending with the foundation of Vienna in 1107. By 1200 there were about seventy fully fledged towns already in existence in south Germany, and almost all of these lay within the ancient Roman territory, and included, with the few exceptions just noticed, all the principal cities of to-day. The overwhelming majority of towns, however, appeared in the later Middle Ages, and by 1400 the basic pattern of the modern road net and almost all the towns were in existence.

The early medieval routes were located in the Bavarian plateau, serving for the transport of salt from the Salzburg district, and in the Rhine plain and the Neckar basin. The Augsburg-Ulm-Mainz route (using the Brenner Pass across the Alps) was the only through main trade route used in early medieval times for German trans-Alpine traffic. This traffic was, indeed, negligible until after 1200, when it grew rapidly and was a main stimulus to the development of routes and towns. The earlier route was then displaced by the Regensburg-Nürnberg route, and the latter city became the focus of a radial system of roads in the eastern area, known as Franconia. The towns of the Rhine plain owed their development above all else to their wine trade, only secondarily to the trans-Alpine trade which was insignificant until the opening of the St. Gotthard Pass in 1232. The main medieval route net in south Germany, instead of being based on through routes of early medieval origin as in north Germany, emerged through the fusion of irregular trackways of local origin, and the great majority of its small towns began as local market centres, industries becoming of greater importance in the later Middle Ages.

Although south Germany is lacking in the bases of modern industry, it includes some of the chief industrial areas in modern Germany. Its industries depend above all on the skill of the workers, and the goods produced are small in bulk and high in value. There has been, in consequence, no great shift in the centres of population, and in general the growth of population in cities and towns in the modern era has been proportional to their medieval importance. The outstanding centres to-day are Frankfurt, Stuttgart, Munich and Nürnberg.

Politically, southern Germany falls since 1815 into the states of Baden, Wurtemberg, Bavaria and Hesse east of the Rhine, while west of the Rhine are the Rhenish Palatinate, an outlying portion of Bavaria, and the provinces of Alsace and German Lorraine acquired by France from the loose association with the old Reich, and regained by the Reich of Bismarck in 1870 and held till 1919. This grouping of political units replaced a chaotic mosaic of divisions that, in the Rhinelands in particular, had persisted since the thirteenth century. Bavaria always has retained the shape of its medieval dukedom, but in 1803 the bishoprics of the middle Main lands were added to it. Bavaria had its nucleus in the old settled area of southern Bavaria south of the Danube between the rivers Lech and Inn. In the centre it included the lands of several secular states—Nürnberg, Ansbach and Bayreuth—and the Upper Palatinate, all of which were mainly Protestant in faith. Nürnberg and its satellites was one of the greatest seats of medieval industry. Finally, in the north the inclusion of the bishoprics of Würzburg and Bamberg in 1815 brought an entirely new element in the Main valley—old settled lands, fertile grain growing country, with productive vineyards all closely related to the Frankfurt area, though separated from it by the barrier of the Odenwald and Spessart uplands. The ancient dukedom of Swabia lay almost entirely in old Roman territory and from the beginning was deeply impregnated with Romance culture. In the thirteenth century it split into a confusing pattern of territorial districts—the lands of bishops, feudal lords of many grades, scattered imperial territories and the free Imperial cities. From this pattern there emerged several outstanding powers, appearing on the map of 1789 as the Free Cities, the Kurpfalz, Wurtemberg, Baden, and scattered Habsburg territories in the south, as well as the bishoprics of Strasbourg, Mainz, and Augsburg, to name but the chief.

The broad features of the distribution of population are indicative of the present economic character of south Germany and provide a basis for the assessment of its regional integrations. The outstanding fact is the belt of high population density in the western section. The Rhine plain is to-day, as always, a great focus of routes in the heart of continental Europe. It is also traversed by the Rhine, accessible for large barges to Strasbourg, the greatest navigable waterway in western and central Europe. It is finally one of the most fertile lands, with very high agricultural productivity. In this trough there is both a high density of rural population and a marked clustering of urban centres. From north to south there are the cluster of towns at the confluence of the Main with the Rhine—with Frankfurt and Mainz-Wiesbaden as the chief centres ; Mannheim-Ludwigshafen-Heidelberg ; Karlsruhe ; Strasbourg ; and Basel, in addition

to a number of smaller towns.   Reference to the population map
shows (Fig. 13, p. 37), however, that the populous areas are not
by any means limited to the Rhine plain.   The latter is flanked
by populous areas in the Neckar basin (Wurtemberg), and is
continued southwards into Switzerland, and there is another outlying populous area in the Saar to the west.   In the Rhine plain
itself, it will be noted that there are two main populous areas,
the Mainz-Frankfurt agglomeration, and the lesser Mannheim-
Heidelberg-Karlsruhe agglomeration.   East of this great populous
block in southern Germany as far as the eastern frontiers, the
rural density of population is much smaller, towns are more
evenly distributed and farther apart, and there are several
dominant centres, the chief being Munich and Nürnberg.

Let us glance at the present agricultural conditions in south
Germany.

The high plateaus of south Germany have a heavy rainfall
and are largely forested.   Patches of cultivated land on stony
soils are devoted to the hardiest and quickest growing crops—
oats, rye and potatoes—which are used both for human consumption and animal foodstuffs.   The valleys contain rich, often irri-
gated meadows, and the higher slopes have rough pastures in or
above the forest, these pastures being especially characteristic of
the Black Forest and the Vosges.   The cattle in these areas yield
less milk than the best dairying areas in the coastal marshes in
north Germany, but this milk contains more butter-fat.   Much
butter and cheese are produced for distant markets.   In the
Bavarian plateau (that is, Bavaria south of the Danube), with its
tracts of cultivated land interspersed with marsh, forest and wide
river meadows, wheat and barley cover considerable areas and are
even sold as cash crops.   Throughout these areas farms are small,
averaging $12\frac{1}{2}$ to 50 acres.   In the Black Forest a particularly
large part (two-fifths) of the ploughed land is devoted to potatoes.

Throughout south Germany there stretches a great triangular
area with its apex in the lower Weser lands, its base on the
Danube, and flanked to east and west by sheltering highlands.
In this area hilly lands alternate with lower lands and valleys.
The latter are mainly arable, since they not only have good soils,
but they are also dry and warm, whereas there is a gradual
mergence into a pastoral economy at higher altitudes.   The
upper limit of wheat cultivation is about 1,000 ft. and of rye
about 2,000 ft.   In these higher lands and everywhere on sandy
soils, rye, oats and potatoes are the chief crops, and, on balance,

livestock exceed crop sales. The basins and valleys are fertile
and sheltered and produce crops of wheat, barley, and even beets
and orchards. Arable land amounts to some two-thirds of the
cultivated area, meadow land about a quarter to a third. The
whole of this zone is one of small holdings with scattered strips,
and subdivision of holdings has been greatly aggravated by the
custom of divided inheritance—a most important factor in the
growth of industrial occupations. The three-field system is
retained over large areas. The peasant and his family do all the
farm work ; a meagre living is wrung from the poor land, and
little is sold. There are few horses, and the cow is at once
a milk, draught and (ultimately) meat animal. Frequently the
farm does not support its workers and supplementary occupation
has to be sought in workshop or factory or by emigration to the
city or abroad.

The lower lands and valleys of south-west Germany form
a very distinctive agricultural region. The Rhine plain and its
flanking valleys—notably the Main and the Neckar—enjoy a small
rainfall and a long warm summer. This is the region of vines,
orchards, tobacco and hops. These are the chief cash crops of
tiny holdings with scattered strips, in which appear, in bright
mosaic, small fields of wheat, maize, and potatoes from which,
and their cows, the peasants obtain their food. The smooth
plateaus of the middle Main and Neckar valleys, with warm
limey soils are good grain-growing country.

The whole of southern Germany falls into three major regions
from the point of view of modern regional integrations, the
so-called Rhine-Main region, the South-west region, and Bavaria.
Let us examine each of these in more detail, emphasizing in each
case the principal unifying characteristics.

II. THE RHINE-MAIN REGION

The nucleus of this region is the great complex of urban
centres at the northern end of the Rhine plain at the confluence
of the river Main with the Rhine. It is, and always has been,
politically divided, but its unity is due to the dominance in the
past, no less than in the present, of its two chief centres, Frankfurt
and Mainz. This region, though having no political unity, is
now generally known—to student and layman—as the Rhine-
Main Region.

Once again, at the risk of being tedious, we must emphasize

the importance of Frankfurt as a focus of routes, for this is the main basis of the integration of activities in the region. The head of the Rhine plain broadens out to include the plains of the lower Main valley, so that there is here a particularly large area of fertile plain. This is surrounded by wooded uplands through · which natural routeways lead out from the plain : the Rhine gorge to Cologne, the only easy route across the plateau and one of the great European trade routes ; the skein of routes going north-eastwards through Hesse between the Middle Rhine Plateau and the Vogelsberg ; up the Main to Würzburg and Nürnberg ; up the Neckar to Stuttgart and, in earlier days, right through to Augsburg and the Brenner Pass—the earliest main trans-continental trade route in Germany ; up the Rhine plain to Basel and across the Alps—in the past via the St. Gotthard pass and to-day by rail ; and south-westwards to Saarbrücken and the Moselle valley in Lorraine.

Mainz and Frankfurt are the historic foci of these routeways. Mainz, situated on the west bank of the Rhine, was a Roman settlement and, as an archbishopric, became both a great trading centre and a cultural outpost. Its connections in the early Middle Ages were predominantly westwards. Frankfurt lies on the north bank of the lower Main. It was chosen as a residence by the Carolingian emperors, for it had a central position in relation to the German settled lands at this time. Its connections, indeed, were primarily eastwards with the German lands in the Carolingian Empire. But it was overshadowed by Mainz and did not become a town until the early thirteenth century. It was not till 1330 that the big fair held at Mainz was transferred to Frankfurt, and from then on, with the development of medieval trade and industry, Frankfurt forged ahead and left Mainz far behind, though the latter remained the seat of the archbishopric. Frankfurt, like Cologne, became one of the greatest centres of commerce and finance in Europe, a rôle which it retains to this day.

The modern era has witnessed the further growth of both industry and commerce and its integration around the Mainz-Frankfurt node. The plains are areas of intensive farming, with vineyards, orchards, market-gardening, and arable crops, grown on minute holdings. Mixed farming and dairying is practised in the lowlands in the wider environs between the wooded uplands. Many of the villages are industrialized and only about a quarter of the occupied population is engaged in agriculture.

Industry depends mainly upon transport facilities and labour resources, only to a very small degree on local natural resources, which, as throughout south Germany, are scanty. Most important are the iron ores of the Lahn and Dill valleys and the iron working grouped around Wetzlar—though these particular industries, as we have noted, are more closely allied with the Ruhr. The chief industries are chemicals, metals and machinery, vehicles, leather and boots and shoes, and none of these depends on local raw materials. Characteristic are luxury goods, such as jewellery at Hanau, leather goods at Aschaffenburg, optical instruments at Wetzlar. Special attention should be given, however, to the heavy chemical industries, the only heavy industries in the region. These are related to coal-tar distillation and draw upon coal and require large quantities of water. The greatest chemical plants are at Ludwigshafen, but there is also a large plant at Höchst near Frankfurt. It may be noted that the leather industries, that are markedly localized in this region, began by using local materials but are now entirely dependent on various imported supplies. The towns of the Rhenish Palatinate are concerned with making boots and shoes and Pirmasens and Zweibrücken are the chief centres. Offenbach is engaged in making leather goods.

From Hanau in the east to Wiesbaden-Mainz in the west there is a chain of towns, the greatest of which, lying in the centre of the chain, is Frankfurt. Hanau (41,000) has jewellery, rubber and cigar industries. Offenbach (81,000), with its leather industries, lies on the south side of the Main and is virtually a part of Frankfurt from the brick-and-mortar point of view. Frankfurt (546,000) has electro-technical and general engineering industries and produces bicycles, motor-cars, and clothing, though it is still pre-eminently a seat of commerce. Höchst and Griesheim lie to the west of Frankfurt and are now included in the city area, and have great chemical industries. Russelsheim (14,000) is the seat of the famous Opel automobile plant. Mainz (159,000) has a variety of industries. Wiesbaden (172,000) lies immediately north of the Rhine opposite Mainz and is connected with the latter by Biebrich to form one " conurbation " ; it is itself a famous health resort with little industry. This whole belt, a chain of centres, rather than one continuous built-up belt, has over a million inhabitants and is one of the chief urban and industrial concentrations in western Germany. This is the nucleus of the Rhine-Main complex.

The significance of this area as a focus of routes is evident in the railway routes, as shown on the maps of passenger and goods traffic (see Figs. 22 and 23). No less than ten long-distance routes commence in either Frankfurt or Mainz, and over 700 trains enter the Central Station of Frankfurt daily. The Frankfurt-Darmstadt *autobahn* was the first to be opened and four of these highways are to converge on Frankfurt, though steering clear of its centre (Fig. 24). Modern industry owes its growth above all to these favourable transport facilities by rail, by the Rhine and by road.

The growth of population in the Rhine-Main region has greatly increased its relations with the surrounding lands, with respect to the spread of suburban settlement and the daily movement of workers to and from the factories and offices, and also in regard to the supply of the cities with their daily food requirements. Indeed, we have here an excellent instance of the organization of circulation around one great urban complex. These varied aspects have been the subject of careful investigations. An investigation [1] of the daily journey to work in this area, published in 1938, revealed total numbers of "commuters" (described as people working in the centre but living outside it) as follows : 28,000 Frankfurt, 6,200 Mainz, 15,000 Russelsheim, 4,000 Darmstadt, 6,000 Hanau and 6,500 Offenbach. Some facts indicated by this study are the overlapping of the commuting areas owing to the closeness of the centres to each other ; the limitation of the journey distance to about one hour in either direction ; the considerable importance of the bus and cycle in the daily movement ; and the remarkably large movement of workers to the great Opel works at Russelsheim between Mainz and Frankfurt. Most of the 15,000 workers working here but living elsewhere come from scattered districts to the south of the Main by bus and cycle. In a study of the movement of food-supplies into Frankfurt, two main areas of supply around the city were determined. The inner area coincides with the most fertile lowland around the city that produces fruits, vegetables and milk supplies. An outer area, with varied physical features and agricultural conditions in its different sectors, consists mainly of wooded uplands and sends varied supplies of foodstuffs from scattered areas to the Rhine-Main centres. From these considerations we can recognize three roughly concentric zones of

[1] See W. Hartke, *Das Arbeits- und Wohnortsgebiet im Rhein-Mainischen Lebensraum,* *Rhein-Mainische Forschungen,* Heft 18, 1938.

influence. The nuclear area is in the form of a triangle, defined by Mainz-Wiesbaden, Frankfurt and Darmstadt, and the areas most closely tied up with them from the standpoint of commuting and the daily movement of workers. All of this area is accessible to Mainz or Frankfurt within one hour and a large part of it within half an hour. It is bounded by the hills to the north, east and west, and by the rival sphere of Mannheim-Ludwigshafen to the south. It has a radius of roughly 50 kilometres from Frankfurt, and its axis is the urban chain we have already noticed. Beyond it is a wider zone, which is the main zone of food supplies drawn to the cities, with satellite towns. An outer zone, much more vaguely defined, is thinly peopled, covering large wooded upland districts, beyond which are rival centres of population and rival cities—the region of Saar-Pfalz to the south, with Saarbrücken and Mannheim as centres ; Hesse to the north (centred in Kassel) ; Siegerland to the north, which is more closely allied economically with the Ruhr, though the Lahn and Dill valleys fall definitely into the Rhine-Main sphere. The Koblenz region is allied with both Cologne and Frankfurt, as we have noted above (p. 75).

In spite of the unity of this region, in the past as well as in the present, it has always been politically divided. With the political disintegration of the thirteenth century it fell into several parts—the bishoprics of Mainz, Worms and Speyer and the *Landgrafschaft* of Hesse in the heart of the region ; and Nassau in the south-eastern sector of the Rhine plateau. From these there gradually crystallized Hesse in the north-east, Würzburg to the east, Kurpfalz in the south (absorbing the bishoprics of Worms and Speyer) ; the bishopric of Trier in the Moselle valley ; and Nassau in the north (though this again split up into several independent territories with the break-up of the dynasty). The territory of the nuclear area belonged mainly to the archbishops of Mainz. After 1866 there were three Prussian provinces, the State of Hesse, the isolated Birkenfeld district of the *Land* of Oldenburg ; and parts of Bavaria and Baden on the margins. Frankfurt itself lay in a small corridor of Prussian territory. To-day, the area within 50 kilometres of Frankfurt is divided between three States (*Länder*), Bavaria, Hesse and Prussia. The last includes the two government districts (*Regierungsbezirke*) of Wiesbaden and Kassel, so that the urban axis itself is seriously divided politically.

All kinds of economic, trade, professional and administrative organizations necessarily cut across these divisions and choose their centres in Frankfurt. There is obviously urgent need for a new arrangement of areas and new powers for purposes of inter-town planning. An unofficial regional planning body was established in the 'twenties and there are various scientific bodies concerned with the investigation of the problems of the region.[1] In the organization of the National Socialist State, the region is recognized as a unit, with the name of Rhine-Main, both for purposes of regional planning and for the organization of the Party, and both of these closely correspond with the area defined above (see Figs. 9 and 10).

III. SOUTH-WEST GERMANY

This region in broad terms includes the whole of Baden, Wurtemberg, the Rhenish Palatinate and the Saar. Although in historical development and modern economic structure it has the same characteristics as the Rhine-Main Region, it is oriented away from the latter around separate centres. Moreover, this whole area has always been closely associated with the trans-Rhine provinces of Alsace and Lorraine, which for centuries were members of the Reich, but passed to France during the seventeenth century, and were later acquired by Bismarck's Reich in 1871, when their present economic character took shape in close association with the Ruhr. Since 1918 they have passed again to France and in some measure reoriented, although there remains the fundamental dependence of the iron and steel industries of the *minette* fields of Lorraine on the coking coals of the Ruhr. After these preliminary comments we shall have no more to say about these two border provinces, though it should always be borne in mind that they have close commercial relations with the Rhine through the river port and economic metropolis of Strasbourg.

Most of the industries of south-west Germany are of recent origin, dating from the mercantilist period of the seventeenth and eighteenth centuries, when the ruling houses sought to give to their States the greatest measure of economic independence or autarky. Some of the domestic industries in the poverty-stricken uplands are old, and, though surviving in part, they have not become so important to-day as in Saxony and Thuringia, where the chief industries had similar origins. The growth of

[1] Such as the *Rhein-Mainischen Forschungen des Geographischen Instituts der Universität Frankfurt-am-Main*. Also the *Rhein-Mainscher Atlas,* edited by Behrmann and Maull.

domestic industry was encouraged not only by royal favours, but also by the laws of divided inheritance, which caused farm holdings to be so sub-divided that they could not give employment to, nor support, a whole family, and other sources of livelihood had to be found by taking up a craft in the home, working for a master in a workshop, or emigrating—and this region was the chief source of German emigration in the nineteenth century. The combination of farming and some cottage craft or work in a factory some distance from the home is to-day one of the most distinctive features of the economic structure of Wurtemberg in particular.

The old industries were predominantly cottage industries. The mechanized industries of to-day developed during the eighteenth century and after within the different states with sheltered tariff barriers, enjoying royal favours and drawing upon the labour of a densely peopled countryside. Industry is thus remarkably widespread in small towns and villages and farmsteads. A very large proportion of industrial workers have small holdings. Women, too, make up a good proportion of the labour supply, and many workers live some way from their homes and have part-time jobs. Next, we may note that the industries are mainly concerned with high-quality goods requiring skilled processing—a necessity in view of the dearth of the raw materials of industry throughout south Germany (except for the Saar). Industries are thus extremely varied, but predominant are the textile industries, and these, in their development and present organization, though specialized by districts, are remarkably interdependent. This applies to the textile industries in south-west Germany, northern Switzerland and Alsace-Lorraine. A brief historical retrospect will emphasize this point.

The oldest centre of the textile industry was around Lake Constance, together with northern Switzerland. The linen industry was important in the early Middle Ages, using local flax, with its chief centres in Constance, Ulm, Augsburg, and Zürich. Cotton was already in use in the fourteenth century, since the area was nearest to the Alpine passes whence came the materials from the East : Constance, indeed, was the headquarters of the trade with the Levant. From here the making of cotton goods spread along the main trade routes to Augsburg and Nürnberg, and then farther afield to Vogtland, Silesia and Saxony, and these later competitors gradually ousted Constance from its former pre-eminence. This district then gave up spinning and weaving and concentrated on the finishing processes, especially dyeing and printing, and these are characteristic to-day. A revival of the textile industries in south-west Germany did not take place until the mercantilist era, when mechanization— meaning the introduction of new machinery using water power— was gradually introduced and many new firms established. In many valleys, especially in the south of the Black Forest, new textile factories were established round about 1800, mainly by Swiss firms and with Swiss capital. The chief attractions were the running water of the swift upland streams that could be used for driving the new machinery, and the surplus labour available for factory work. To-day, southern Baden is the second greatest silk textile producer in Germany, although silk is still less important than the original cotton products.

The textile industries of upper Alsace grew up about the same time and under the same conditions. They were again of Swiss origin, having their chief seat of origin in Mülhausen. Basel had hitherto supplied this city with cloths for its dyeing and finishing factories ; both of them were in Switzerland with no tariff barrier between them. But after 1798 Mülhausen became politically independent of Switzerland and its industrialists began to establish their own spinning and weaving mills in upper Alsace, using the water power of its streams in the southern Vosges. During the whole of the German period after 1870 this area remained oriented towards France.

Two other districts acquired textile industries in this period. In the Bavarian district of Swabia around Augsburg, the old finishing industries were revived, using water power, and after the 'thirties spinning and weaving also became important. This industrial district has spread to include the Austrian district of Vorarlberg and extends into Wurtemberg. In the Neckar basin, water-power was used along the northern edge of the Rauhe Alb—the seat of an early cottage linen industry—though here weaving and spinning are dwarfed by knitted goods and em- broidery. This accounts, as in Saxony, for the survival of the cottage worker in this district.

While the textile industries have their origins, though far removed, in the Middle Ages, almost all the other industries date from the mercantilist and modern periods, and were attracted by the available supply of labour, which was both cheap and highly skilled. About 1700, clock-makers from Bohemia introduced this craft in the Black Forest. It began as a cottage industry, using local wood, but metal soon began to be used and this, albeit in small quantities, had to be imported from elsewhere. A period of crisis intervened in the early nineteenth century, when the market was flooded with cheap American clocks and royal intervention caused the introduction of mechanized processes in factories. The chief centre is Schramberg and around it, in Baden and Wurtemberg, are four-fifths of the clock-workers in Germany. Closely allied with the clock-making industry is the making of musical instruments (harmonicas) around Trossingen. These industries together are dominant throughout the south-east of the Black Forest and the south-west of the Rauhe Alb. The making of jewellery began, and was localized, by chance. Hanau has been noted as a centre in the Rhine-Main Region, but the chief centre is Pforzheim, the greatest centre in the world.

The production of machinery, vehicles, etc., is usually distributed widely in all towns, and is often related to a main industry, supplying its machinery, e.g. textile machinery in Saxony. But in south-west Germany there are two engineerng industries that have grown to special importance, and owe their location to chance and the availability of a labour supply. These are the automobile and airship industries. We need only mention the names of Daimler of Stuttgart and Zeppelin of Friedrichshafen. Another special industry is the manufacture of electrical supplies and appliances, for which Stuttgart is an outstanding centre. Finally, the cigar industry began in the last century in two districts, around Heidelberg and Offenburg, as an aid to a distressed rural area, where there was a surplus of labour owing to the excessive subdivision of farm holdings.

The only heavy industry in south-west Germany is connected with the Rhine. We have already noted the great cluster at Ludwigshafen-Mannheim on the Rhine front, using coal and water in the distillation of the coal. There is a second district, centred at Waldshut and Rheinfelden on the Rhine. This owed its start in 1880 to the nearness of salt deposits ; this advantage passed with the change-over from the Leblanc to the Solvay process in the preparation of soda, the chief basis of the alkaline chemical industries, and the modern development is due to the use of hydro-electric power derived from the Rhine. At the source of generation, great temperatures are available for special kinds of smelting and for electrolytic processes in the production of alkaline chemicals. The same factors account for the localization of aluminium smelting at Rheinfelden, which, though in Swiss territory, is based on German capital.[1]

The Saar coalfield and industrial area, with its 864,000 inhabitants, is a special district and has special problems. The district lies in the Saar valley on the northern border of Lorraine and adjacent to the German province of the Rhenish Palatinate, and about midway between the Lorraine iron-fields and the Rhine, with its ports of Strasbourg and Mannheim-Ludwigshafen. The coalfield produces about 13 million tons per year : the French section to the south-west has produced about 6 million tons in recent years. In addition, there are produced about 2 million tons of pig-iron and 2 million tons of steel and $2\frac{1}{3}$ million tons of coke. The field lies in a narrow belt running north-east to south-west for about 15 miles with Saarbrücken, the capital, in the Saar valley, at its south-western end. The Saar valley contains the chief iron and steel plants at Saarbrücken (135,000), Völklingen, Saarlouis, and Dillingen. As in Upper Silesia, the iron industry concentrated here in the nineteenth century in order to be near both fuel and ores. With the advance in technology, ores were soon inadequate, and had to be obtained from Lorraine, and the local coal, though excellent for gas coal, is useless as coke for modern large ovens. So that the furnaces require a coke from the Ruhr or elsewhere, or a coke made by mixing local coal with coal from the Ruhr and Holland. The industry stays where it is because of its invested capital. The Saar developed, then, in the 1870–1914 period in the closest relation to the Lorraine-Ruhr complex, and was thoroughly integrated in the Reich economy. According to the Treaty of Versailles the coalmines and iron and steel plants were passed to France for a period of fifteen years. During this period the economy of the Saar was completely reversed and by various tariff devices was absorbed into the French system.[2] By its return to the Reich this process must be again reversed and the territory reincorporated in the Reich. This process was under way before the present war.

About one-third of the coal production of the Saar is absorbed on the field in home and factory. In 1913 three-quarters of the

---

[1] Only since the last war has the smelting of aluminium been located at other places in Germany, where great heat can be obtained at the point of production of electric power, namely, in the lignite fields of Central Germany and Lower Lusatia and, more recently, in the Inn valley where hydro-electricity is used.

[2] The difficult transition period was helped by permitting the free entry of German goods for five years. In 1925 the frontier was closed. This applied also to Alsace and German Lorraine.

export of 4 million tons went to Germany—to Alsace-Lorraine, Rhenish Palatinate and south Germany (mainly for the production of gas). Since the last war about 4 million tons have gone to France, and only 1 million tons to Germany, where the south German market has been supplied from the Ruhr. The bulk of the coal has thus been marketed in France, and the iron ores drawn from the Lorraine field, which became French after the war.[1] Moreover, the supply of consumption goods was in large measure shifted from the German to the French market. Goods traffic with Germany in 1913 was about 2½ million tons, and with France was negligible, as compared with about 1 million tons with Germany and half a million with France (an additional half-million with Alsace-Lorraine) in 1925–30. It is quite impossible to estimate the changes that took place after the return of the Saar to Germany in 1935.

The connections of the Saar with the Rhine are by rail and one canal. The latter was built in the 'sixties to join the Rhine-Marne canal and link the field with the Rhine system·at Strasbourg. This is inadequate and there have long been German plans for the construction of a new canal direct to Ludwigshafen-Mannheim. Indeed, the close relation of the Saar to the Palatinate and Mannheim is evident from the traffic statistics, for about a half of all its trade with south Germany is with the Palatinate and this port.

Modern regional integration is effected primarily by circulations, and these, as we have just indicated in the case of the Saar, can be basically altered by a change of political frontiers. But in south-west Germany the regional associations effected by commerce and the journey of persons to work show clearly the interdependence of the various parts of the region and its unity as a whole. The relations between the States are as significant as the local movements within them.

The direction and intensity of commercial relations may be judged from the movements of workers, and by traffic by rail and water. This region, and especially Wurtemberg, is the classic region of local *Pendelverkehr*—the daily movement of workers over considerable distances, by rail, bus and bicycle, from home to the factory. Especially noticeable here is that in Baden there is very little settlement on the Rhine plain. Villages and towns are clustered at the foot of the Black Forest and in the Black Forest itself. The latter lie but a few miles from the Wurtem-

---

[1] In 1928 about a half of the pig-iron and of the steel was marketed in Germany.

berg districts and there is a good deal of movement of this kind over short distances across the Baden-Wurtemberg frontier. The chief centres of this movement are Mannheim and Pforzheim on the Baden side and Heilbronn on the Wurtemberg side. On the other hand, Ludwigshafen on the west bank of the Rhine draws heavily on the Palatinate for its workers. But the greatest amount of local movement takes place in Wurtemberg itself, and the chief focus of movement is Stuttgart.

The railway goods traffic in 1932 of each of the six traffic districts of south-west Germany with the other five is given in the following table, together with the proportion this regional traffic bears to the total traffic of each district with the Reich as a whole.

District	Million tons Regional Traffic	Percentage of Total with Reich
Wurtemberg	4·1	54·6
Baden	3·9	47·7
Mannheim-Ludwigshafen . . .	3·6	43·5
Bavarian Palatinate	2·0	75·7
Hesse	1·2	23·7
Saar	1·1	53·9

The grand total of this regional traffic amounts to 16 million tons. Three-quarters of it consist of industrial goods, the chief being coal (6·4 million tons), stones and earths (3 million tons), minerals and chemicals (1·2 million tons), and iron and steel goods (0·75 million tons). Among the remaining quarter, made up of agricultural and forest products, timber is the bulkiest item. Several points should be emphasized in this traffic. Note the relatively small proportion (25 per cent.) and amount (1·2 million tons) of the traffic of Hesse with the south-west—this province is focused on Frankfurt and its relations are mainly northwards. Note also the overwhelming orientation of the Palatinate to Ludwigshafen-Mannheim. Of its regional traffic (i.e. the total with the other five districts), nearly 40 per cent. is with this centre, 20 per cent. is with the Saar and 15 per cent. with Hesse. The large bulk traffic of Ludwigshafen-Mannheim arises from its importance as a river port and trans-shipment point for distribution and collection in the south-west (Bavaria, and to a smaller degree, Switzerland), and from its heavy industries (chemicals, metals, timber and paper). In this respect, Mannheim has one important rival in Strasbourg, whose river traffic has increased since the improvement of the Rhine upstream and since the restoration of Alsace and Lorraine to France :

both are served by the French river port. The bulkiest product passing through the port of Mannheim is coal, two-thirds of which comes upstream from the Ruhr, with the balance drawn from the Saar. Coal makes up 60 per cent. of its total traffic in industrial goods with the six districts listed above, mineral oils and chemicals coming second with 20 per cent. The Saar, in spite of its orientation to France, has continued to send coal in smaller quantities to south Germany or to Mannheim.

It will be clear from these facts that the provinces *west* of the Rhine—the Rhenish Palatinate, the Saar, and the French provinces of Alsace and Lorraine—have a great deal in common in their economic development, their history, and their dependence on the Rhine waterway through the ports of Mannheim, Ludwigshafen and Strasbourg. To the south, Mülhausen and Basel have been independent centres, affecting the economic development of the territory around them in three states. The close connections between the Saar and the Palatinate that we have emphasized are further evidenced in their combination as one *Gau* in the original pre-war Nazi Party organization and as a Planning Region. We should, however, also note that this region grouped on Mannheim has close relations with both the Rhine-Main Region (Frankfurt) and the South-west (Stuttgart). As a regional focus, Strasbourg ranks with the other great cities of southern Germany—Frankfurt, Stuttgart, Nürnberg, and Munich—and the Swiss city of Zürich, and were it not for the political frontier its sphere of influence would undoubtedly extend over much of south-western Germany, as well as the provinces west of the Rhine. Strasbourg lies at the head of navigation on the Rhine and, as a French port, serves as a back-entry into eastern France, Alsace and Lorraine. It is favoured by various tariff devices and enjoys the same privileges as the sea-ports of France. It shares in the traffic of the Rhine with Mannheim. Basel lies above the effective head of navigation and is not regularly accessible to river barges owing to the swiftness of the current and the seasonal irregularity of its flow. It is not surprising, therefore, that the Nazis have combined the original Saar-Pfalz Region with Lorraine to form the *Gau* of Westmark, and have joined Alsace with Baden, while Luxemburg to the north is joined with Koblenz-Trier to form the *Gau* of Moselland.

The essential unity of the lands of south-western Germany together with the French provinces of Alsace and Lorraine is a point of view that has been emphasized by a German town

planner of repute, and we give his view without any comment.
" The unity of the left bank and the right bank of the upper
Rhine area (*Oberrheingebiet*) is a fact arising from geographical,
morphological, hydrographic conditions ; from the race, speech
and culture ; and from traffic relations and economic development." The political divide appeared with the Napoleonic wars
since when to the political has been added an economic divide.
" A regional plan for the Upper Rhine Region, working outwards
from the river, must recognize both banks as a unit." Drainage
areas must apparently, according to this writer, be the basis of
the planning unit, " from the Rauhen Alb and the Frankenhöhe
in the east to the Côtes Lorraines in the west." This would
include, the writer continues, Alsace-Lorraine and French Lorraine, that is, the Departments of Haut Rhin, Bas Rhin, Moselle
et Meurthe ; and Rhein-Pfalz, Regierungsbezirk Trier, and Basel
and Baselland. Detailed regional studies are needed on the lines
of the atlas of Alsace-Lorraine published at the University of
Frankfurt. The writer suggests that a Regional Planning
Authority be established to cover the whole of this area irre-
spective of political frontiers, and indicates the need for the Saar-
Mannheim canal and the regularization of the Rhine and road
development in the plain as planning matters of the first priority
for common action.

IV. BAVARIA

It has already been noted that politically and culturally the
State of Bavaria forms a separate entity in the south-eastern
sector of the Reich. Its limits are fixed to east and south by
the frontiers of the Reich. To the west against Wurtemberg,
the boundaries follow the Iller to the south and the Franconian
Jura in the west, and to the north the fertile core of the Main
upland is enclosed by wooded hills.

In Bavaria there are three small industrial districts on its
edges that are closely related in type to those in adjacent districts.
These are the textile district of the Vogtland in the north-east,
that is closely related to Saxony ; Swabian Bavaria in the south-
west allied with south Baden ; and the district of stone and
kaolin quarrying in the Fichtelgebirge in the north-east that is
allied with the Thuringian complex and the Central German
region. These are, indeed, the main industrial districts of Bavaria.
Elsewhere the country is dominantly rural except for a few

industrial " islands " in the cities. The chief of these are Munich and Nürnberg. Munich, a great capital city in the heart of the rural plateau of southern Bavaria, has mixed consumer industries. The chief of these, found elsewhere in many small towns of southern Bavaria, is brewing. Important in recent decades has been the development of scattered lignite deposits in the plateau, which, together with the water-power resources of the Alps, serve large electric power plants, that provide southern Bavaria with most of its power as well as serving a wider area by connection with the main electric grid system in the Rhinelands. The smelting of aluminium has also been introduced in the Inn Valley.

An entirely different complex is found to the north of the Danube centred on Nürnberg (431,000). This city was in the later Middle Ages the chief industrial and commercial centre in southern Germany, and, on the routes radiating from it like the spokes of a wheel, small towns grew up as its industrial satellites. The skilled metal working industries of medieval times are reflected in the present character of the city and its satellites such as Fürth, Weissenburg and Schwabach. The manufacture of metal wares—made from precious metals and non-ferrous metals—is still most important, including in particular the making of toys. The pencil-making industry may also be mentioned. Like other big cities with good railway communications, Nürnberg has also been chosen as a site for various heavier engineering industries, these industries being located in large plants on the southern outskirts of the city, while the older industries are carried on in numerous small workshops and factories in the old town. Elsewhere, the many small towns have industries of purely local significance. Bamberg is an isolated centre of textile industries, Würzburg and Schweinfurt have engineering industries, the last, as we know from recent bombing raids, being the chief centre in Germany for the manufacture of ball-bearings.

Munich dominates the life and economy of southern Bavaria. It is the ancient and modern political capital of Bavaria and its greatest industrial and commercial centre. Situated in the midst of the thinly peopled plateau, with its coniferous forests, heathland, marsh and stretches of fertile, cultivated land, it is the fourth city in Germany with 828,000 inhabitants in 1939—not far short of a million if its contiguous towns and villages be included. Its industries, like those of other historic regional and political centres, are extremely varied. That only 40 per cent.

of the population is dependent on industry (which is about the average for the whole of the Reich) is evidence of its main importance as a centre of the other regional functions—commerce and administration. Together with health and domestic services these groups of occupations account for 27 and 15 per cent. respectively of its population.

Thus, in Bavaria, the permanence of the political pattern, the contrasts in economic development and present characteristics between the southern plateau centred on Munich, the central hills and basins centred on Nürnberg, and the northern fertile plateau and valley of the Main, centred on Würzburg and Bamberg, the marked differences in rural economy, political development and cultural associations, permit us to recognize three main divisions the extent of which is primarily determined to-day by the dominance of two main cities, Munich and Nürnberg, which have no rivals. The whole of Bavaria is taken as a unit for purposes of regional planning under the Nazi scheme, but for Party organization the distinct units within it find expression in the four *Gaus* of Main-Franken, centred on Würzburg, Bayrisch Ostmark, that includes the whole of the thinly-peopled forested uplands, Franken that is centred on Nürnberg, which is in effect also the dominant centre for the previous unit, and München-Bayern centred on Munich. East of this the Augsburg district, known as Schwaben, recognizes the historic separateness of this area from Bavaria and its closer affiliations with the South-west.

It will be appropriate, in concluding this section, to emphasize the fundamental unity of what are vaguely described as the Rhinelands. This unity is based on a common orientation of drainage and principal traffic flows towards the Rhine ; on a common basis of culture and political development ; and on the interdependence of its specialized economic sectors as evidenced by their historic development and their present needs. In respect of modern economic traits there should be emphasized the two great industrial areas of the Ruhr and Lorraine with the Saar and their independence on each other and on the Rhine waterway ; and the common economic development of the lands on either side of the upper Rhine—the South-west and Alsace and the Rhenish•Palatinate. It is upon the great inland navigable artery of the Rhine and its tributaries and the lowlands centred round them, that the human unity of these lands is based. The fertility of its soils, and its wealth of natural resources, are reflected in its very high density of rural populations, and its many large urban agglomerations. Two historic cities, each a great modern agglomeration, dominate the Rhinelands—Cologne and Frankfurt. Basel too has a geographical situation favourable to the growth of a great city, although it lacks the advantage of navigation on the Rhine whose effective head of navigation is at Strasbourg. For this reason, though probably in the main because the political disintegration of the upper Rhinelands left Basel on the frontier of Switzerland, with the regional functions divided between Mühlhausen, Strasbourg and Mannheim, this city has not attained great size. The whole of the Rhinelands, in the broad sense, consist, it will be noted, of three German regions—the Rhineland-Westphalia, Rhine-Main, the Southwest, the transitional province beyond the Reich borders of Alsace-Lorraine, and Switzerland to the south.

CHAPTER VII

CENTRAL GERMANY (MITTELDEUTSCHLAND)

I

In recent years the term Mitteldeutschland has been variously applied to the whole or part of the densely populated and highly industrialized lands of the middle Elbe basin, south of Magdeburg. The close network of routes, the active interchange of goods between its complementary parts, the dependence of the whole area upon brown coal or lignite as its main source of fuel and power, and the dominance of several large cities, knit this whole area into an entity. It so happens that this entity contains an outmoded pattern of political divisions which is a hindrance to the smooth working of its commerce and administration. Moreover, the demands of long-range physical planning in respect, for instance, of the extensive lignite fields and the industry and settlement associated with them, as well as the need for creating more rational administrative units, have prompted in the last twenty-five years numerous studies of the economic character of this area and the inter-relations of its parts. The middle Elbe basin, however, is of special interest not only as illustrating excellently the idea of a geographical unit, and the problems of defining it; but also on account of the development of an entirely new industrial complex based upon its lignite and salt resources and of vital war industries—electric power, chemicals, aircraft and precision instruments—due to its central position in the heart of Germany.

The great belt of high population density which stretches across western and central Europe has its most extensive and most populous area in the centre of Europe, lying astride the frontiers of Germany and Czechoslovakia. In Germany this forms a large triangular area in the middle Elbe basin, with its base along the Czech frontier and its blunted apex between the Harz and Magdeburg.

The southern boundary of this area is the German-Czechoslovak frontier. In spite of the fact that this frontier follows the summits of the Erzgebirge, there is, in fact, no break in the density of population, and the populous industrial areas on either side of it in Saxony and Bohemia form parts of one great population block ; it is the political frontier that for centuries has determined

the contrasts between them. To the north and east there is a sharp
break in density against the marshy plains of the Schwarze Elster
and the Elbe and the Ohre and Aller valleys west of Magdeburg
(the route followed by the Mittelland Canal) ; while beyond are
thinly-peopled rural expanses of heath and forest covering uplands and marshy valley floors of the North German Lowland.
To the west, the populous area includes the uplands of the Thüringerwald and beyond lie more thinly-peopled rural areas in the
wooded uplands of the Fulda and Werra basins. In this direction
the border is without clear linear definition on the basis of population densities, but it is clearly revealed as a broad zone between
two series of towns, Halberstadt, Nordhausen, Mühlhausen and
Eisenach, all of which are tied up with the Mitteldeutschland
complex, as against Kassel, Göttingen, Goslar and Brunswick,
which belong to the complex of Niedersachsen (Lower Saxony).

This triangular area has its corners in the Görlitz-Bautzen
district of Silesia to the south-east, the Hof district of north-
eastern Bavaria to the south-west, and the foreland of the Harz
and the Magdeburg *Börde*, merging into the territory of Brunswick to the north-west. These broad facts of population distribution provide a basis for the recognition of this area as a
natural human unit. But there are variations of density and
distribution within it which correspond to variations of its
economic structure. Five great cities, each with over about
200,000 inhabitants, dominate the economic life and organization
of the whole area : Leipzig (701,000), Dresden (625,000), Chemnitz (334,000), Magdeburg (334,000), and Halle (220,000).
Smaller towns, with 100,000 to 200,000 inhabitants are Erfurt
(166,000), Plauen and Dessau, and not far below this limit are
Gera, Zwickau and Görlitz. There are about thirty towns with
between 20,000 and 50,000 inhabitants. The greatest population clusters are grouped around Chemnitz, Dresden and Leipzig.
Small towns and ancient centres equally spaced on old trade
routes are characteristic of Thuringia and the lowland between
Halle and Brunswick. From these facts we may deduce, on
the one hand, that this unit is distinct from its neighbours by
virtue of its high density of urban and rural populations, its high
degree of industrialization, its close network of routes and great
intensity of traffic ; and on the other hand, that within the unit
there are markedly contrasted regions, that are likely to be complementary and therefore interdependent.

The whole region has an area of about 50,000 square kilometres (20,000 square miles) and about 10 million inhabitants. It has just over a fifth of all the industrial workers in the Reich and accounts for just under a fifth of the installed power. This compares with an area of 40,000 square kilometres and 12 million people in Rhineland-Westphalia, which account for the same proportion of workers but over double the power.

Let us glance at the broad features of the physical build of the middle Elbe basin. It is framed by, and includes, to the south and west, the wooded uplands of the Erzgebirge and their extensions and the Thüringerwald, and the isolated block of the Harz uplands in the north-west. These uplands are generally hilly or rolling in surface and merge gradually in slope and drainage into the lowlands. The latter are bounded to the north by large stretches of flat, marshy land, forming an arc from the Elbe valley below Dresden to Magdeburg and its westerly continuation in the Aller valley. North of this trough are the heath and forest of the Fläming and Lusatian uplands of Brandenburg. The lowland falls into two sectors. The Thuringian basin in the west lies between the Thuringian uplands and the Harz. It has circular belts of hills and an open fertile core centred on Erfurt. Wooded plateaus, crossed by the Saale in the east, separate it from the plains of the so-called Leipzig Bay. This is flat, open, treeless arable country, merging into wooded and partly cultivated uplands to the south in Saxony, and stretching northwards around the Harz and southwards at the elbow bend at Magdeburg towards Brunswick. It is bordered to the north by the marshy plains of the Elbe.

Central Germany lies at a great crossways of routes. In the past, overland routes from west to east and from north (North Sea and Baltic ports) to south (Frankfurt and Nürnberg) crossed the area, using the relatively easy passes across its encircling uplands. The natural focus of these routes lies in the heart of the Leipzig Bay, and here Leipzig came to be its greatest city. It is only in the late nineteenth century that its pre-eminence as a route centre has been usurped in some degree by Halle, a still more historic centre of the area. This was developed as a railway centre in Prussia in opposition to Leipzig, that lay only a few miles away, but inside Saxony, at that time a separate and independent kingdom. For this reason, Halle is still the chief railroad centre and Leipzig has inadequate direct connections with Berlin.

The rich arable soils of the Leipzig Bay form the heart of an agricultural region which stands in marked contrast to the neighbouring lands on all sides. A large area with over two-thirds of the total land devoted to arable cultivation lies between a northern line from Brunswick to Magdeburg and the Elbe plain from Magdeburg almost to Dresden to the north ; and a southern line due west from Dresden including the Unstrut basin, as far west as Mülhausen to the south. The proportion actually reaches 80 per cent. between the Harz and the Elbe and 70 per cent. in the Leipzig Bay. From this great nuclear area, with an economy based on sugar beet, wheat, barley and stall-fed cattle, the proportion of arable land falls rapidly on all sides, to 35–50 per cent. in the lowlands north of the Elster-Elbe-Ohre trough, and decreases to only 20–35 per cent. in the uplands to the south and west, where woods and meadow play a dominant rôle in rural land use and economy.

Special problems of land development arise in these rich arable lands through the recent exploitation of the lignite beds which underlie them, and the growth of heavy industry, problems which involve a compromise between the demands of farming and industry. Great areas of the richest soil in Germany have been destroyed to make way for lignite quarries ; villages have been cleared ; and the disused quarries put to profitable use again. There are problems of the disposal of industrial refuse, the pro-vision of water and power to the plants, and the distribution of electricity by overhead and underground transmission lines. There are also the problems associated with the migration of farm workers to the factories, the daily movement of workers, and associated transport and housing problems ; and there are the problems of taxation to support these new areas, and the question of the proportionate distribution of the burden of taxa-tion as between farmer and factory worker. Hence the urgent need for planned, rather than fortuitous, land development. In the field of planning, especially important are the maps and proposals, based upon an elaborate investigation by a voluntary regional planning body in 1932, of existing conditions in the lignite-producing region around Merseburg.

II

The political development of the middle Elbe basin reveals the fact that while for centuries much of the area was controlled by the kingdom of Saxony, this gradually broke up for dynastic reasons, resulting in the independence of the Thuringian states, while the southern expansion of Prussia gradually whittled down the territories of Saxony, reducing them in 1815 to their present frontiers.   The result is the complexity of the present political map, entirely detrimental to the modern development of the whole area as an effective human unit.

In the early Middle Ages Central Germany was a frontier province, bisected from north to south by the political and cultural barrier of the Elbe and the Saale rivers.   Under the Carolingians this was the eastern boundary of the Reich and the divide between the spheres of German and Slav settlement.   Along this river frontier a series of fortress towns, serving as trading centres and bishoprics, overlooked the Slav lands to the east.   The part of the Frankish province of Thuringia west of this line was con-trolled from the archbishopric of Mainz, and that east of it from the archbishopric of Magdeburg.   In the tenth century the whole area east of the Saale was divided into the three frontier provinces (or marks) of Nordmark (Altmark), Ostmark (Lusatia), and Thuringia.   The last was again divided into the marks of Merseburg, Zeitz, and Meissen, each territory being centred on the town of that name.   The first two were shortly after merged in the mark of Meissen, which became the nucleus of the Wettinian dynasty and of their kingdom of Saxony, while Altmark became the nucleus of the Hohenzollern territories of Brandenburg out of which grew Prussia.   The political fate of central Germany stems from these two powers.

The Wettinian dynasty, appearing in the eleventh century in Saxony, gradually extended its territories, and reached, at the end of the fifteenth century, from the Werra to a line west of and parallel to the Elbe and from the Erzgebirge to a line from Mühlhausen to Wittenberg—approximately a rectangle in shape. A University was established at the great commercial centre of Leipzig in 1409 and the Fair in 1497.   But in 1485 their terri-tories, by a split in the dynastic line between the two brothers Ernst and Albert, were divided into two parts, from which there emerged the group of small states in Thuringia and the kingdom of Saxony.   The Hohenzollerns gradually extended their territory southwards from 1648 onwards, and in 1815 Prussia absorbed all the Wettinian (Saxon) lands north of Leipzig and most of Lusatia, which territories were formed into a new province of Prussia called Saxony.   This " geographical monstrosity," as it has been called, has its administrative capital in Magdeburg, and

Merseburg and Erfurt had other administrative functions. Halle has a university. Only Anhalt remained as an independent political unit. Though appearing as a geographical anomaly Anhalt has persisted with little territorial change from the thirteenth century onwards, with a strong tradition of unity among its people, maintaining its independence between the two great rival powers of Saxony and Prussia. After the great territorial changes of 1815, there were seventeen independent sovereign states in central Germany. These were reduced to twelve in 1866, though there was little change in frontiers. In 1920 the State of Thuringia was formed by the union of a number of small " ruritanian " states—the dukedoms of Sachsen-Weimar-Eisenach, Sachsen-Meiningen, Sachsen-Altenburg, and Sachsen-Koburg-Gotha (without Koburg), Schwarzburg-Rudolstadt, Schwarzburg-Sondershausen.

To-day, there are four states—Prussia, Saxony, Thuringia, and Anhalt—and small outliers of Brunswick in the north-west. The Prussian province of Saxony takes up the northern half of the area, north of a line from Erfurt and Leipzig with southern prongs in Erfurt and Weissenfels-Zeitz. In it there are 'outliers' of Brunswick (Blankenburg) and Thuringia (Sondershausen). The most extensive 'inlier' is the State of Anhalt, which stretches from Wittenberg in the east to Quedlinberg in the west and lies between Magdeburg and Halle. Erfurt lies in the middle of Thuringia from which it is severed in administration although it is the natural, historical and geographical capital of that province. On the other hand, Sondershausen, belonging to the State of Thuringia, lies in the middle of this Erfurt district. Ziegenrück in Frankenwald and *Kreis* Schleusingen and Schmalkalden in Thuringia, belong to the *Regierungsbezirk* of Erfurt.

Prussia has fourteen outliers in Thuringia (population 130,000), fifteen in Brunswick (population 2,400), and four in Anhalt (population 1,400). There are six outliers of Thuringia in Prussia (82,000), one in Bavaria (5,000). There are twenty-seven small outliers of Brunswick territory in Prussia (169,000). Anhalt has six outliers in Prussia (35,000). This interlocking of territories, each having separate administrations, and yet all bound together by the facts of modern economy, is the cause of the great attention given to the problem of the " natural " geographical units in the middle Elbe basin.

III

In the middle Elbe basin there are great contrasts in economic structure between Saxony and Thuringia on the one hand, and the northern section, consisting of the Prussian province of Saxony and the State of Anhalt on the other. The distribution of the principal industries is shown on Fig. 28.

At the end of the Middle Ages, say in 1500, the northern section, covering the fertile forest-free lands, was an exclusively agricultural area. Two minerals were mined from early medieval times in and around the Harz, salt and copper. The southern section, Saxony-Thuringia, for the most part hilly and wooded and infertile, was settled in the Middle Ages for the exploitation of its iron and silver. Mining and smelting reached their peak in the fifteenth and sixteenth centuries when a number of new towns were founded, including Annaberg. In the north, this general picture did not appreciably change during the ensuing two centuries, but in the southern half there were important changes. The kings of Saxony were able to foster industry to an extent which was impossible in the scattered small territories of their cousins in Thuringia. With the decline of mining and smelting, the textile industries, as cottage industries, became of increasing importance throughout the countryside. In Thuringia, similar domestic industries grew in the uplands, together with woodworking, and the making of glass and porcelain ; whereas the lowland remained agricultural and industry was confined to the towns. In the nineteenth century the small coalfield of Zwickau gave a further fillip to industry in Saxony, although until the advent of lignite as a fuel, running water was the main source of power for workshop and factory. Alongside the textile industries grew the manufacture of machinery and chemicals. Thus Saxony, to-day the most densely populated major province of Germany, is much more industrialized than Thuringia, but the two regions have essentially the same character, in that they have highly skilled industries, dominantly textiles and metal working, drawing their material from elsewhere, and some old industries which still depend primarily upon the presence of local raw materials.

Throughout the greater part of Thuringia, Saxony, Anhalt and the southern part of the Province of Saxony, the majority of the people are dependent on industry, and therefore it is in regional differentiations of industry that we are to seek a primary

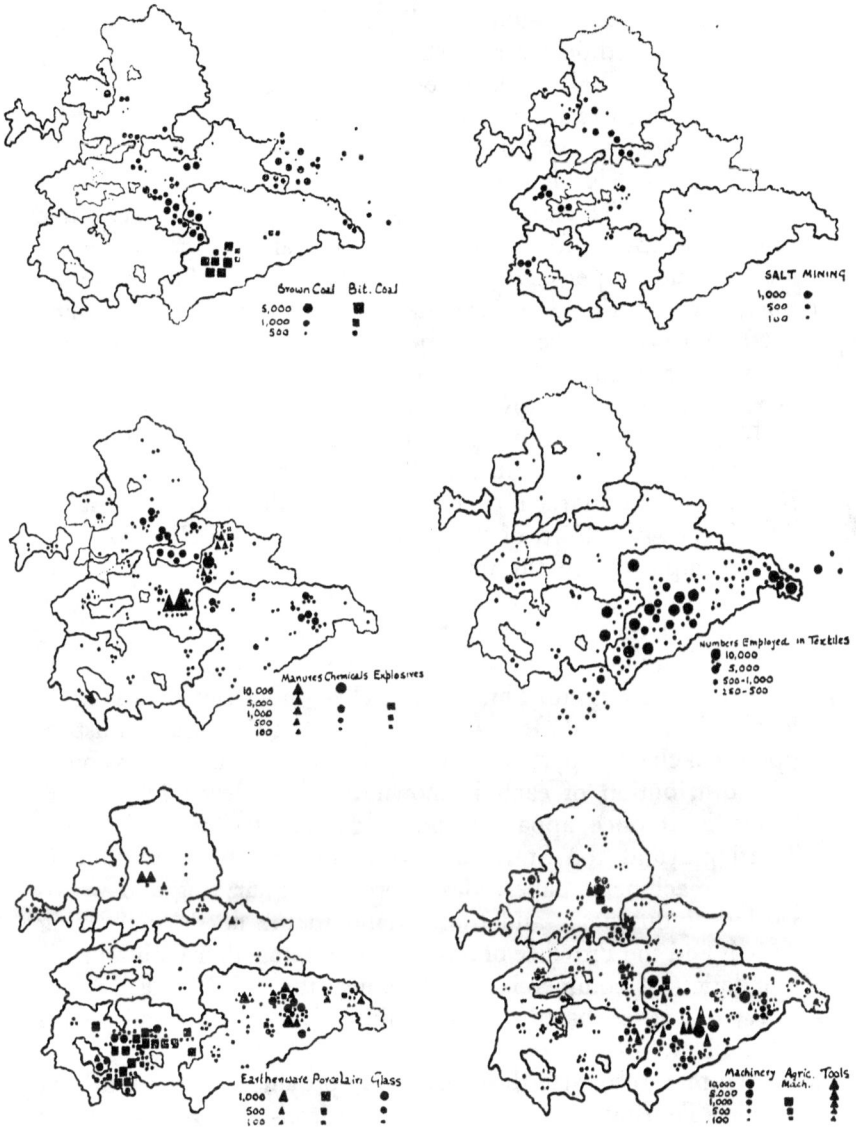

FIG. 28.—The Distribution of Industries in Central Germany.
Numbers of employed persons in 1925.
(After Thormann and Staab.)

F

division into economic units. Indeed, the proportion of the people dependent on industry is highest in the south, in Thuringia and Saxony, and decreases northwards, where, in the Magdeburg *Börde*, over a half depend on agriculture. The metal and machine industries are dominant in each State, aggregating about a quarter of the population employed in industry. Textiles (together with clothing) occupy a third of the industrial workers in the State of Saxony and a fifth in Thuringia. Chemicals and mining occupy a fifth in the Province of Saxony, 15 per cent. in Anhalt, and 10 per cent. in Brunswick, but are relatively unimportant in Thuringia and the State of Saxony. The " stone and earth industries ", like the engineering and textile industries, give a special economic character to the southern half of Central Germany. They occupy a good tenth of the industrial workers in Thuringia, and about 5 per cent. in each of the other divisions. Saxony has nearly a third of the earthenware workers in the Reich, with a marked concentration in the Bautzen district. Thuringia has a third of the porcelain workers. Glass working is also important in the former area. The chemical industries and the mining of brown coal and salts are localized mainly in Anhalt and the province of Saxony. Paper and woodworking are especially important throughout the State of Saxony and the latter also extends into Thuringia. These industries are all highly localized in Central Germany, and they are the basic industries upon which the pyramid of its economic structure is built. The distribution of each is shown in more detail in Fig. 28. There is at once apparent the fundamental contrast between Thuringia and the State of Saxony on one hand with their textile, machinery, paper, glass, porcelain, quarrying and woodworking industries ; and the lowland to the north, embracing Anhalt and the Province of Saxony, where, together with a broad foundation of commercialized farming, the chief industries are heavy industries, based on the mining of brown coal and potash salts.

We may recognize three economic provinces in the southern section (Thuringia and Saxony), where iron- and metal-working and the textile industries are dominant, differentiated by economic structure and orientation around separate cities.

(1) The economic unit of West Saxony and East Thuringia includes the Kreise of Gera and Greiz and the Prussian Kreise of Zeitz, Weissenfels and Naumburg, the western border corresponding with the wooded uplands that are crossed by the river Saale,

where there is a sharp break in the density of population and west of which neither population nor industry is so concentrated. This province specializes in the metal and machine industries and is the chief producer of textile goods in Germany. Its chief towns are Leipzig, Chemnitz and Plauen, and Leipzig is its capital.

(2) East Saxony and Upper Lusatia are centred on Dresden. The principal industries are metal-working, chemicals (photographic and pharmaceutical products) ; glass-making in the coalfield on the edge of the Erzgebirge (Lugau-Ölsnitz) ; paper-making on the Elbe. The eastern Erzgebirge is oriented both economically and geographically towards Dresden, whereas the Flöha valley is more closely allied with Chemnitz. The linen and more modern cotton industries in Upper Lusatia are centred in Görlitz and Lauban, and at Zittau and Löbau in the extremity of Saxony. The historic unity of the Lusatian area is reflected in the past confederation of its six chief cities. The industry is fed by the Lusatian lignite. East of Görlitz, economic character changes and both industry and population densities fall off. To the north the boundary is formed by the frontier of Brandenburg along the belt of heathland. Dresden (625,000) is the centre of an urban industrial area which extends from Meissen to Pirna. It is surrounded within a few miles by a number of small towns with 25,000–50,000 inhabitants in which heavy industries are characteristic, whereas Dresden, the " garden-city " of Germany and the political capital of Saxony, is a centre of miscellaneous light industries, heavier industries being located in its south-eastern outskirts.

(3) Thuringia between the Harz and Thüringerwald (and including the latter) has its capital in Erfurt, situated in the centre of the area, although it lies in an outlier of Prussian territory. This is mainly an agricultural lowland with scattered small towns, very ancient in origin and to-day specialising in light, skilled industries. Especially notable are the series of towns, strung at equal distances along old routes, like beads on a chain, through the Goldene Aue to the north, and the series running east–west through Erfurt itself. Industry is more widespread in the Thüringerwald, and the density of population higher than in the lowland though the soil is far less productive and in large measure is forested. Metal-working, glass-making, toys, porcelain, are its chief industries. Jena is the centre of the Carl Zeiss works.

The latter half of the nineteenth century had witnessed an

industrial revolution in the Prussian province of Saxony and in
Anhalt. Industry appeared with characteristics directly opposite to those of the south. It grew in the first place from the
local agriculture and from local natural resources. Lignite was
used in a small way as a domestic fuel in the eighteenth century
but its large-scale exploitation followed upon the growth of the
sugar-beet industry in the 'thirties, on the model farms of the
area when fuel was needed in the sugar-beet factories. Then in
the 'sixties salt-mining began and lignite was used for the industries which grew up in association with it. In the 'seventies
the briquetting process extended the field of delivery and the
variety of its uses as a fuel. The distillation of lignite commenced
in the 'fifties and other processes for its treatment rapidly
followed. Through low-temperature carbonization of lignite
is obtained tar, from which is distilled benzine, oil for diesel
engines and paraffin for tallow. Nitrogen is also extracted from
the tar in the form of ammonia, which is used for the manufacture
of fertilizers. Vast electricity plants, drawing lignite direct
from the quarries, have been erected, and supply central Germany and Berlin with the bulk of their consumption. The chief
lignite-producing areas are the districts of Bitterfeld and the
Geiseltal, both being in the *Regierungsbezirk* of Merseburg, with
Halle as its centre. There are extensions of the producing area
to north-west Saxony, around Leipzig, and part of the Altenburg
district.

The development of other large-scale chemical industries
was further facilitated by the proximity of potash salts. The
production of these commenced in the 'fifties near Stassfurt,
where they occur with rock salt, though till this time the potash
salts had not been used. The latter are now the more important.
Since these salts contain only 20–40 per cent. of pure potash salt
they must be processed before they can be used as fertilizer, and
for this large quantities of fuel are needed. This is obtained from
the neighbouring lignite quarries, and since the 'sixties lignite
has been used on a large scale for this purpose. Chemical
industries using both salt and lignite, and located near the latter,
have grown since the 'nineties. The Bitterfeld lignite field is
the chief centre. These industries made a great leap forward
during the last war with the manufacture of gases and explosives, using nitrogen extracted from the air. Vast works
appeared at Bitterfeld, Wittenberg and Leuna. The chemical
industries have continued to grow in the inter-war period

(1918–39) producing soda, chlorine, nitrogen, tar, artificial silk, photographic products, etc. The chief seats of potash salt production have now shifted west to north-western Thuringia and Hesse. To-day the chemical industries consume a third of the lignite production.

It is characteristic of this new industrial area in Province Saxony and *Land* Anhalt that though its industries are mainly heavy industries, the plants are relatively few and very large and are grouped around or near to the lignite quarries, in the midst of one of the richest agricultural areas of Germany. The population is clustered around small medieval towns and in new workers' settlements near the plants. Nearly all these urban settlements are small, with under 50,000 inhabitants. Examples of the first type are Bitterfeld and Wittenberg ; and of the second the Leuna works near Merseburg. The whole area is served by the navigable Elbe and by a network of roads and railways. Its principal centres are Magdeburg, at the elbow of the Elbe where land routes converge on a city that is a great river port and industrial centre ; and Halle, which is accessible by small barges from the Elbe, but is primarily a railway focus. Magdeburg is undoubtedly the principal commercial centre for the area north of the Harz and for Anhalt. Along the south side of the Elbe, above Magdeburg, there is a series of small river-port towns, which have attracted large-scale industry owing to their favourable location. The chief of these industries are chemical works, sugar factories and engineering works, to which must be added the great Junkers aeroplane works at Dessau, which now has well over 100,000 inhabitants. The towns are Schönebeck, Kalbe, Aken, Köthen and Dessau. Between the Elbe and the Mulde, south of the Dübener Heide are Bitterfeld (chemicals), Zschornewitz (power plant) and Eilenburg.

Province Saxony and Anhalt and the adjacent areas in Thuringia, Saxony and Brunswick to the north, form an entirely separate and distinctive industrial area of modern development, a distinction, as we have already seen, that also applies to agriculture and types of countryside. This area lies between the Harz and the Fläming Heath, with its economic centres in Magdeburg and Halle. Its essential character is shown by the combination of open, highly productive farm land (wheat, sugar beet), and large-scale industry—lignite (brown coal) quarries and potash salts with attendant brickworks, sugar-beet factories, chemical works and electricity plants. Halle is the geographical focus of this area which includes the *Regierungsbezirk* of Merseburg and the *Land* of Anhalt. Its limits are not clearly defined, and it merges gradually into Brunswick and the Leipzig Bay, where its typical industries are mixed with others. The political frontier is in many ways an artificial, but a real divide, separating this region from Saxony. The northern section, north of the Harz, includes ancient towns and old metal-working centres which, historically, have been closely associated with *Niedersachsen* to the west, but economically are dragooned in particular towards the river port and rail centre of Magdeburg.

IV

There are, then, deep-rooted contrasts in the economic development and the present character of the industries as well as of agriculture between the northern and southern sectors of Central Germany. The whole area, however, is a homogeneous unit in respect of four main characteristics in its circulations and organization—the close network of through and local routes ; the old-established interchange of goods between its parts, which is now so important, in comparison with trade with other areas of similar extent in the Reich, as to mark it off as an integrated commercial unit ; the fact that to-day brown coal, the chief item in bulk in its railway traffic, gives a basic unity to the whole, since, with the lack of coal and water-power, brown coal—in the form of briquettes or of electricity—is almost the sole source of domestic fuel and of power for industry ; and, finally, the dominance of the largest cities over local circulations, economy, and organization. These cities are Leipzig, Dresden, Chemnitz, Magdeburg, Halle, Erfurt and Plauen, with Leipzig as the focal city, the greatest in size and its chief commercial and cultural centre.

Central Germany produced in 1927-28 nearly a half of the production of brown coal in Germany (Thuringia-Saxony, 35 per cent., Upper Lusatia, 5·0 per cent., Brunswick-Magdeburg, 5·0 per cent.), whereas Lower Lusatia supplied 22·5 per cent., and the Lower Rhineland (west of Cologne) 28 per cent. Brown coal deposits underlie the rich agricultural plains and are known to form a north–south oval-shaped area, with Leipzig at its centre, extending 40 kilometres from east to west through Leipzig and 70–80 kilometres from north to south, with many outliers on the western edge. A second area, a long thin belt, running north-west-south-east to the north of the Harz has its chief centre of production, in Helmstedt. Production is localized in several separate districts which overlap into all of the main administrative divisions in the region. The chief producing areas are in the heart of the region.

Coal production is limited to the State of Saxony at Zwickau, Glauchau and Stollberg, which produce the small amount of 4 million tons per year.

. Lignite, amounting to nearly half of Germany's total produc-. tion (three-quarters if Lower Lusatia be included), is the bulkiest commodity in its traffic, making up 27 per cent. (about one-third with coal) of the traffic of Magdeburg-Anhalt, 41 per cent. (nearly a half with coal) of that of Merseburg-Erfurt, and about a third (40 per cent. with coal) in each of Thuringia, Saxony and Leipzig.[1]

As regards receipts and despatches for each district for both coal and lignite, Central Germany, considered as these five traffic provinces, is a closed province to the extent of 70 per cent. of its trade. The percentage of all rail traffic of each district with the other four districts in Central Germany is : Magdeburg-Anhalt 42·7, Merseburg-Erfurt 49·8, Thuringia 59·8, Saxony 49 and Leipzig 75. Thus, 51·6 per cent. of the total traffic of these five districts is with each other, and the remaining 48·4 per cent. with the rest of Germany.[2]

These districts, with the exception of Leipzig, are large and their size obscures the orientation of some of their area to neighbouring districts. In this respect, attention is drawn to the relatively densely-peopled industrial districts, in which Mitteldeutschland tapers out to north-west, south-east and south-west. The lowland north of the Harz, in so far as it is oriented towards Magdeburg, and is a lignite-producing area (around Helmstedt), may be included in Mitteldeutschland. This would seem to be supported by both features of relief and natural vegetation as well as by the industry and agriculture of to-day. Nevertheless the whole area has close ties with Brunswick, and includes detached sections of that State, and has considerable trade with

[1] These districts refer to the official traffic districts used for railway returns (*Verkehrsbezirke*). They are *Regierungsbezirk* Magdeburg and *Frei Staat* Anhalt, *Regierungsbezirk* Merseburg, R.B. Erfurt, and F.S. Thuringia, F.S. Saxony, and Leipzig and district. For details on lignite trade, see H. Thormann and F. Staab, *Der Mitteldeutsche Raum*, 1929, p. 75.
[2] Thormann and Staab, op. cit., pp. 160–5.

Niedersachsen (Hanover). All writers and proposals are agreed that Brunswick itself should be excluded from Mitteldeutschland. The Hof cotton manufacturing district, lying on the south side of the Thüringerwald, is closely allied with both Mitteldeutschland and North Bavaria. The Görlitz (in Silesia) and Zittau (in the extreme corner of Saxony) districts are similarly transitional to Silesia, though beyond them there is a definite break in the density of population and industrial intensity. Lower Lusatia, though a lignite and textile industrial area, is closely allied functionally with Brandenburg and Berlin, so that the Brandenburg frontier may be taken as the boundary against Central Germany.

As regards water transport, the Elbe itself is the only deep, navigable river, and it borders the whole of the northern and eastern margin of the area. It is now continued westwards by the Mittelland canal, which joins the Elbe a few miles below Magdeburg. There are no other waterways of any importance south of this route, and break-of-bulk points on the Elbe are fed by road and rail. The Saale alone is navigable by small barges to some miles above Naumburg (200 tons) and barges of 1,000 tons can now go as far as Trotha, below Halle.[1]

Magdeburg is the great river port for northern Mitteldeutschland, but, as noted above, there are several small towns east of it, on the south bank of the river, which are important trans-shipment points for goods coming up and down the Elbe and are also, in consequence, seats of heavy industry.

There is a high density of traffic and of routes per unit of area in the middle Elbe basin. In general, this reflects, as we might expect, the distribution of population, and the radial arrangement of local routes brings out clearly the location of the spheres of influence of the small country towns, especially in Thuringia. Most remarkable is the very high density of routes, and the heavy traffic on them, in the whole of the Erzgebirge in Saxony from Upper Lusatia to Plauen and Hof at the western end. This broad zone passes, by a gradually wider spacing of density lines, into the Halle-Leipzig Bay, although the close network of routes is a main feature, narrowing northwards from the Saxony base to Magdeburg and the country on the northern slopes of the Harz westwards to Brunswick, and, without a break, to Hanover.

---

[1] Canals are planned to link Gera and Leuna to Leipzig and Torgau and the Saale is to be canalized to link Merseburg (Leuna) with the Mittelland Canal. The building of the barrage on the Saale will also regularize the flow of water.

The density of the route net and of traffic decreases abruptly to the north beyond Magdeburg and the Elbe. Thuringia has a distinct pattern with its equally-spaced old towns, each with a radial road net dominated by Erfurt, and there are many short local routes feeding the industrialized Thuringian uplands. A recent study of all categories of traffic circulations calculated on a density basis for twenty-nine districts reveals some interesting facts about Central Germany.[1] Five districts correspond with this area. The high density in the State of Saxony and the south of the Province of Saxony is due to the density of the railway net in very populous areas. But the upland areas around this have a highly developed road net as well as a close railway net, for they too are densely populated industrial areas with high traffic " potentials ". This applies to the Harz, Thüringerwald, Frankenwald, the Fichtelgebirge and Erzgebirge. Here road services make up for the inadequacy of railway facilities. Thus, the " Thüringerwald, Frankenwald, Fichtelgebirge " district, according to this authority, combining both a close railway and road net, exceeds the rest of Central Germany in its traffic density, and stands third only in the Reich after the Ruhr and the Cologne Bay. The Harz also has a higher density than the Thuringian lowland. But these conclusions are based on the density of traffic *routes*. The density of *traffic* using them reveals that the greatest intensity of traffic is in the State of Saxony, and the south of the Province of Saxony, that is, in the great urban and industrial areas.

This brief survey reveals in broad terms the intrinsic characteristics of the middle Elbe basin in respect of the distribution of its agriculture, industry and population and its commercial circulations. The fact that these distributions and space relations cut across political divisions means that both the student and the organizer or administrator must adopt new " natural units ". It is thus no wonder that this unit as a whole figures, with variations, in the numerous nation-wide divisions of the Reich and in regional associations, and that innumerable proposals by both public authorities and private investigators have been put forward for " natural " or homogeneous geographical units, as economic groupings inherent in the structure of modern society. It is of interest to note, in conclusion, that in all these regional definitions, the Leipzig-Halle area figures con-

[1] H. Ende, *Die Verkehrsdichte des Deutschen Reiches, Archiv für Eisenbahnwesen*, Hefte 3 and 4, 1936.

sistently as the heartland. The border areas with divided allegiance are Hof in northern Bavaria and Görlitz in Upper Lusatia in the south-west and south-east corners of the region, and the Magdeburg region in the north. The last is in many ways a distinct area, and the thinly peopled heathland just north of Magdeburg in the Altmark is almost unanimously excluded from Central Germany. But though the focal point of a distinct closely settled area north of the Harz, Magdeburg itself as a great river port and industrial centre serves the Saxony-Anhalt industrial and agricultural area, it has close relations with Berlin and Hanover, and it is equidistant from these two and from Leipzig-Halle and Hamburg. Thus, the Magdeburg area is a transition area between the important regional nuclei around it. The same sort of transitional character is found in Lower Lusatia, which, as a new industrial area, is allied to both the Central German region in its brown coal interests, and to Berlin in the marketing of its products and its administrative organization.

CHAPTER VIII

THE BALTIC PROVINCES : NORDMARK, POMERANIA, AND EAST PRUSSIA

These provinces extend along the shores of the Baltic Sea. They include, from west to east, the chief political divisions of Schleswig-Holstein, Mecklenburg-Strelitz and Mecklenburg-Schwerin, Pomerania, and beyond the Polish Corridor—the former German province of West Prussia—East Prussia, an isolated outlier of German territory.

This tier of provinces corresponds with a distinct belt of country that is bounded to the south by a great arc-shaped trough of flat land, along which flows the lower Elbe, then, in northern Brandenburg, the trough is followed by a canal to the lowest angle of the Oder, and thence along the Warthe-Netze valley to the lowest angle of the Vistula at Bromberg. Beyond this point, on the southern confines of East Prussia, the trough is followed by the Vistula and its eastern tributaries, the Narew and the Bobr rivers. Between this trough and the coast there is a belt of country, about 100 kilometres wide, in which there is a broad belting of types of country parallel to the coast and the trough. First, there is a stretch of level and usually fertile land behind the sand spits and enclosed lagoons of the coast, a zone that is very closely cultivated, with nearly all the land under arable crops. Then follows a zone of hummocky country, with numerous shallow depressions, with lakes, marsh, and large areas under coniferous forest. Thirdly, on the south side of these hills and intermingled with them, there are stretches of level land, with infertile sandy soils on broad valley floors, the greater part of which is forested or marshy. This in turn gives place to the flat valley trough to the south. Three wide plains, traversed by the lower courses of the chief rivers, break this whole belt into three blocks. The plains are those of the Memel, which is more or less continuous with that of the Pregel, bounding East Prussia on its eastern side; the lower Vistula; and the lower Oder. There is no clearly defined river break in the west, but the isthmus between Hamburg and Lübeck is flat and narrow.

Historically, this whole belt beyond Kiel was brought into the sphere of German settlement in the Middle Ages, from

1150 onwards. In the west, Schleswig-Holstein was, in fact, part of the area of original German settlement in the lands west of the Elbe, and has close cultural affiliations with *Niedersachsen*, as, for instance, in dialect and house types. The medieval " colonized land " begins east of Kiel. The Slavic Wends were subdued in the twelfth century and Adolf of Schauenburg founded Lübeck in 1143, the first *Kolonialstadt* to be established in northern Germany. Then followed the conquest and settlement of the eastern provinces in the thirteenth century, while the conquest and christianization of the lower Vistula and East Prussia beyond was left to the Teutonic Knights. Along the coast, ports were founded in quick succession, in general eastwards from Lübeck, all sharing in the Baltic trade and drawing traffic from their hinterlands, and all being members of the Hanseatic League of which Lübeck was the leader. In Pomerania and East Prussia, in particular, there was a good deal of intermixture with the native Slavs. In East Prussia, Masurian (Polish) dialects, and in West Prussia (now the Polish Corridor), the native Polish speech of the primitive Kassubes, have persisted in spite of rigid Prussianization. Moreover, the absorption of these more easterly provinces into Prussia was tardy, for Polish influence was strong after the downfall of the Teutonic Order until the partitions of Poland at the end of the eighteenth century. Facing the Baltic Sea, these provinces were associated with the fate of its dominant sea-power. Thus, with the end of the Hanseatic hegemony, power passed in the seventeenth century to Sweden under its great leader Gustavus Adolphus, and the Treaty of Westphalia in 1648 awarded western Pomerania (*Vorpommern* as opposed to *Hinterpommern* east of the Oder) to Sweden, and it was not until the early eighteenth century that this territory was returned to Prussia. Pomerellen (later known as West Prussia) and East Prussia were virtually Polish territory until the partitions at the end of the eighteenth century.

Throughout the centuries down to 1789, there were several distinct political units in this area. In 1789 there was Holstein to the south and Schleswig north of Kiel, the latter a border province, never closely affiliated with the first Empire. Neither province was effectively incorporated into Prussia until their conquest in 1864. At the neck of the peninsula, bordering Holstein, were the Free Cities of Hamburg and Lübeck with their territorial outliers in the isthmus, together with the old dukedom of Lauenburg and several other small territories. To

the east of these were the dukedoms of Mecklenburg-Schwerin
and Mecklenburg-Strelitz ; then between the northern boundary
of Mecklenburg and the Baltic coast, the province of *Vorpommern*,
attached to Sweden till 1720 ; and the dukedom of Pomerania
east of the Oder. We may note here two prongs of Brandenburg
jutting northwards, the Uckermark, almost reaching Stettin, and
the Neumark to the east. Finally, West and East Prussia lay to
the east, acquired by Prussia in the Polish partitions. In 1815
this framework of units remained on the new map, Pomerania—
Vor and *Hinter*—becoming a single province of Prussia. The
chaotic grouping of interlocking territories in the Holstein
isthmus was recently cleared up by a Nazi decree. . Lübeck loses
its status as an independent State and is absorbed into the Prussian
Regierungsbezirk of Schleswig. The many outlying villages that
were outliers of Lübeck, designed formerly to protect the trade
routes and to assure Lübeck's food supply, are also absorbed
partly into Schleswig and partly into Mecklenburg. Further
along the Mecklenburg-Prussian border there is a general
elimination of outliers that date from the fourteenth century.
The Eutin district, formerly under the control of the bishops
of Lübeck, passed to Oldenburg in 1803.

The whole of this Baltic belt is predominantly agricultural,
with small country towns and only a few large towns, all of which
are ports. In all the provinces, except Schleswig-Holstein, the
proportion of people engaged in agriculture alone exceeds the
proportion in industry and commerce combined. The density
of population is also the lowest in the Reich ; large areas in
Mecklenburg and Pomerania and in the interior of East Prussia
have densities of population well under 100 per square mile.
The most populous areas are found in the Hamburg-Lübeck
isthmus and in the lower Oder. There is, moreover, a marked
similarity in the type of farming throughout the belt in spite of
secondary contrasts. The similarity lies in the fact that the whole
belt specializes in stock production and is the chief area of
surplus production and export in the Reich. The rolling countryside with fertile soils—similar to those of East Anglia—next to the
Baltic coast is predominantly arable, while forest dominates in
the hilly interior, and meadow and grasses in the coastal marshes
of western Holstein. Holdings are generally large (except in
Holstein) and in this respect are highly distinctive as compared
with the rest of the Reich. Mecklenburg, in particular, is the
land of the Junker landlord with estates often exceeding

1,000 acres, and holdings normally having over 250 acres. On the arable land, rye usually exceeds wheat, the latter being more important in eastern Holstein only, and potatoes are grown in combination with rye. Beet is grown on the most fertile soils in Mecklenburg. It is thus a zone of dairying and beef and pig production and it will be remembered that the Holstein farmers gave the impetus to the development of dairying in Denmark. Little fluid milk is marketed owing to the considerable distance from the large urban markets, but large quantities of butter and cheese are exported. This whole range of dairy and stock production is greatest in Holstein and least intensive, with a much greater proportion of waste forest and marsh land, in East Prussia. Berlin draws heavily on these surplus agricultural products, although supplies are delivered to Hamburg from Holstein and throughout eastern Germany.

Towns are small, commerce is local, and large areas are far removed from railways, this again being typical of the whole belt except for Holstein. Moreover, the main routes are concerned primarily with traversing the belt, and the chief cities are ports concerned with transit traffic as well as with the marketing and processing of products from the interior. Thus, these rural areas have a diffuse network of commerce with main traffic arteries crossing them to and from the ports, and large areas lie well outside the effective reach of the latter. The political divisions are thus the best basis for assessment of regional unity, although some obvious changes are indicated, especially the need for clearing up the territorial mosaic in the Hamburg-Lübeck isthmus. The northward prong of Brandenburg (Uckermark), which penetrates Pomerania almost as far as Stettin, is more closely related to Pomerania geographically, and its agricultural activities are like those of the arable lands of west Pomerania.

Three main groupings, it may be noted, are usually used in the division of this part of Germany for many practical purposes, namely, the so-called Nordmark, which combines Schleswig-Holstein, Lübeck and sometimes Mecklenburg ; Pomerania ; and East Prussia. The Nordmark has an area of about 32,000 square kilometres and a population of 2½ millions. Schleswig-Holstein, however, forms a very distinct historical unit and its modern development and interests, apart from its agriculture, have always been closely associated with the commercial and strategic importance of the isthmus crossing from the Baltic to the North Sea. It is also a region essentially of peasant farmers and is old

settled German land with, however, a long tradition of semi-
independence of Germany and of Denmark, though with close
affiliations with both. Dairying is highly developed both on the
marshes on the western coast and on the drier and more fertile
arable land on the east coast, and it has very large surpluses of
all types of stock on farms of 50 to 250 acres in extent. Moreover,
lying across the isthmus, its history has been closely tied up with
that of the ports on the eastern coast and Hamburg at the mouth
of the Elbe. Mecklenburg, on the other hand, is an ancient
Slav province in which the large Junker estate is dominant, with
a semi-servile peasantry living in villages and small towns, and
marketing its agricultural surpluses chiefly in Berlin. Rostock
is the only town to near the 100,000 mark. Pomerania, also an
ancient Slav dukedom east of the Oder, has only emerged in the
last hundred years as a single province and owes much of its
modern unity to the dominance of Stettin. East Prussia is
a clearly defined province geographically, with a history of its
own, an outpost of the Reich and of Germandom, with a very
strong Polish strain in its people as well as in its history. It is
to-day served by Königsberg which has no rival.

It will be clear that in these Baltic provinces regional associations are diffuse owing to the dominance of agriculture and the
small country market town, and to the relative unimportance of
industry. Moreover, from the economic point of view, they may
be regarded as one major province. The main political divisions,
however, have been permanent and between them there are
contrasts in cultural and historical development and modern
rural economy. There is also considerable differential integration of regional activities in the large city ports, which are also
the chief seats of industry. These cities are Kiel and Lübeck,
the small towns of Wismar and Rostock, Stettin, and Königsberg.

Particular interest, then, attaches to these German Baltic ports
which are also, without exception, the principal cities in the
Baltic provinces. In contrast to the port facilities on the North
Sea coast, that are almost entirely confined to the two main river
estuaries (Emden being a foundation of the last decade with the
opening of the Dortmund-Ems canal), the Baltic ports are many
and ancient in origin and are situated either on river estuaries
or in riverless bays. Lübeck, the first to be established as a
German port in 1142, was followed in the thirteenth century by
a series founded to the east of it, ending with Memel, founded
in 1252. The prosperity of these ports in the Middle Ages was

associated with the eastward spread of German colonization beyond the lower Elbe, and the trade with Scandinavia and Russia. This trade was the monopoly of the Hanseatic League with its headquarters in Lübeck—a trade in timber, tar, wax, honey, furs and fish, and, above all, herrings and timber. In the seventeenth and eighteenth centuries, grain from the Baltic provinces of Germany and the interior of Poland and west Russia was added. The Baltic ports were the chief suppliers of grain and timber to western Europe until late in the nineteenth century; and the greatest of them in the eighteenth century was Danzig. In 1850, though Hamburg was the chief German port with shipping tonnage entries reaching over 500,000 tons, Stettin (207,000 tons), Danzig (187,000 tons), Memel (160,000 tons), and Königsberg (127,000 tons) all exceeded Bremen (123,000 tons), and even the smaller ports (Rostock, Kiel, Wismar and Stralsund) continued to handle considerable shipping (from 25,000 to 50,000 tons each). The relative decline of the Baltic ports came after the 'sixties, but there has been in fact a steady increase in traffic. Thus, in 1850 the shipping entries in aggregate to the Baltic ports were 1,500,000 tons as compared with 1,100,000 tons to the North Sea ports. In 1930 the totals were 9,700,000 tons and 34,100,000 tons respectively.

The development of the ports of Schleswig-Holstein reveals clearly the importance of the isthmus location between the Baltic and North Seas. There are several small ports in the deeply embayed coast-line, but only two of these are to-day of any importance, Flensburg and Kiel. Lying at the head of their bays, these small ports were within easy reach, by short overland crossings, of the lower Elbe and west Germany, and they were also connected at the head of the bays by the old north–south route to Denmark, which is now followed by the railway to Copenhagen. Schleswig (20,000 inhabitants) was a port in early medieval times, but was soon superseded by Lübeck and ceased to function as a port at this early date. Flensburg (65,000 inhabitants), founded in 1150, is both a port and an industrial centre. Situated at the head of a bay and at a focus of routes in fertile country, it has always been a port, and in the nineteenth century it acquired industries and became a Baltic shipping centre. But in the twentieth century, and especially since 1919, when the Danish frontier was brought to its doors, the port has greatly declined and is now only of local importance.

Kiel is situated near the head, on the western side, of one of the finest bays. Built originally as a competitor to Lübeck, it grew slowly, joining the Hanseatic League in 1363. But, in spite of a canal built across the peninsula in 1777–87, Kiel remained insignificant in the nineteenth century with only 7,000 people in 1810. The change came at the end of the nineteenth century with the building of the Kiel-Altona railway, the first Baltic-North Sea railway connection (1843–4), the growth of its University (founded in 1665), in connection with the political movements in the two provinces, and above all with the establishment of the naval base after the annexation by Prussia of Schleswig-Holstein, which meant the building of wharves, ship-building yards, new railways and roads and a rapid increase of population, and the growth of its Baltic commerce. The Kaiser-Wilhelm canal (1887–95) did not have the favourable repercussions on Kiel that were anticipated. Though the purpose of this canal was primarily strategic, it served in fact to divert shipping from the Baltic direct to Hamburg, short-circuiting the Baltic ports. Through the depletion of the German fleet since 1919, Kiel has also gone through hard times in the last twenty years.

Lübeck is situated on an island near the mouth of the small river Trave and is easily accessible to the lower Elbe, like its neighbour Schleswig, which it soon superseded. In the thirteenth century Lübeck became the head of the Hanseatic League and controlled the movement of traffic in and out of the Baltic Sea. The zenith of her power was reached about 1500 when her population numbered over 50,000. In order to carry salt from the Lüneburg district (for the salting of fish in the Baltic ports), the townsmen of Lübeck had a canal built—the Stecknitz canal—the first to be built in Germany (1391–8), to a branch of the lower Elbe, over a distance of 21 kilometres. A second canal was built shortly after 1500 to serve for the transport of general merchandise from Lübeck to the Elbe, but this, as a joint undertaking of Lübeck and Hamburg, soon fell into disuse through difficulties of water supply and the opposition of the landlords, through whose territory it passed. The need for these two cities to control the Elbe-Trave corridor led in the Middle Ages to territorial conflict with the small feudal lords between them and to their obtaining control of scattered bits of land which still appear on the map, though most of these have been eliminated, as noted above. There was, indeed, one small district in which, until 1868, the administration changed hands between Lübeck and Hamburg every seven years. In the course of the sixteenth century came the decline of Lübeck, while Hamburg throve. The dominion of the Baltic passed from the Hansas to Denmark and then to Sweden, and the Dutch mercantile marine took over much of the Baltic carrying trade in the seventeenth century. Further, there came the great shift of commerce from northern Europe to overseas. The revival of Lübeck did not take place until after 1870. The Trave navigation was improved, a new harbour was laid out below the old town, the Elbe-Trave canal was built, and opened in 1900, following the course of the old Stecknitz canal, and new industries were introduced—blast furnaces at the mouth of the Trave (using Swedish ore, Gothland limestone and English or Upper Silesian coal), as well as oil mills, chemicals, engineering and timber yards and timber working. In 1939 the population was 153,000.

Wismar (30,000) and Rostock (122,000) are the two chief towns of Mecklenburg and both are small ports, and always have been small, for they cannot compete with the isthmus location of Lübeck nor with the river location of Stettin. Rostock has an old University dating from the eighteenth century and has a small shipbuilding industry. About 10 kilometres downstream is Warnemünde where there is a train ferry service from Berlin to Sweden. At Rostock there are extensive aircraft works. The two places together have well over 100,000 inhabitants.

Stettin lies midway between Flensburg and Memel at the head of the marshy estuary of the Oder. It is the farthest inland of the Baltic ports and the nearest Berlin, with which it is connected by rail and water. Beginning as the capital of the Slav province of Vorpommern, on the west bank of the estuary, it became a German town in 1243 and entered the Hanseatic League in 1360. After the Middle Ages Stettin declined as a port in spite of the fact that the Oder basin was now a closely settled German land in Brandenburg and Silesia. This was because Stettin and Pomerania were cut off from this natural hinterland. Until 1637 Pomerania was independent and then, with the end of its dynastic line, it fell to Sweden, so that Brandenburg and Silesia directed their commerce westwards to the Elbe. This was the reason for the building of the Friedrich Wilhelm canal (1662–9) between the Oder and the Spree to connect directly Silesia, Berlin and Hamburg and to side-track Stettin. Frederick William II acquired Stettin and the Oder estuary in 1719–20 and part of Vorpommern to the Peene river at the mouth of the Oder. In 1815 the rest of the province was acquired by Prussia.

The barriers were thus removed and Stettin's development began. The Finow canal was built between the Oder and the Havel (1740–6) and the Plauer canal linked Magdeburg and Berlin. Sweden still controlled the Peene mouth of the Oder at Wolgast in the early eighteenth century, so Frederick the Great founded Swinemünde at the outlet of the Swine, which could take larger ships than Stettin and was ice-free for a longer period. This became the outport of Stettin, until the navigation up to Stettin was improved to take vessels up to 10,000 tons in 1880. The modern harbour has been built on the marshy islands on the east bank of the river opposite the town. In 1816 Stettin had 24,500 inhabitants—about the same as Lübeck and half the size of Danzig ; in 1939 it had 267,000 inhabitants. Stettin is thus the biggest German Baltic port and industrial centre. Ship-building is old established ; blast furnaces were founded in 1895, using Swedish ores, and English or Silesian coal, and other industries are timber and paper, and oil-milling, with cement, bricks and sugar-making as secondary industries based on local raw materials. It also has become a chief outport for Berlin, especially since the opening in 1914 of the Hohenzollern canal that takes 600-ton barges.

Königsberg dominates the trade of East Prussia. With a population of 368,000 in 1939, it is far less important as a port than Stettin or even Lübeck. The large size of the city is due to other causes : it is the seat of government of East Prussia, the economic and cultural focus of the whole province, and a great garrison centre. It lies not far from the mouth of the river Pregel on the Frisches Haff, and is at the last easy crossing above the marshes flanking the estuary. It is also 40 kilometres from Pillau on the Baltic coast and a similar distance upstream by canal to the Kurisches Haff which leads to Memel. It thus lies at the head of the river estuary, at an outstanding bridge point, in a central position as a market for the closely settled countryside. Königsberg was the headquarters for the conquest and settlement of East Prussia. The Hanseatic merchants controlled the trade in timber and grain and its trade monopoly reached from Memel to Danzig. Its University was founded in 1544. Decline came about 1600, due to conflicts with Danzig, the attacks of the Swedish Gustavus Adolphus (who occupied Pillau and stopped all trade from the port), fires and epidemics, and the partition of Poland, after which Russia sought to divert traffic to Libau, Mitau and Riga. A new period of prosperity came in the middle of the nineteenth century. There were several distributaries of the Pregel, but the main channel was gradually embanked and deepened. The town is situated on the north side of the river and the port on the marshy land on its south side below the town where large areas are reserved for industry on the northern bank below the town. A ship canal was built between 1894 and 1901, 30 kilometres long, cutting through the Haff to Pillau. The latter grew rapidly, after the opening of the canal, as an outport, but since 1919 the trade has declined again, for the hinterland is now restricted to the local traffic of East Prussia and Pillau is now a winter port and summer bathing place (10,000).

The peculiarity of the pre-1918 trade of Königsberg was its large exports of agricultural products from East Prussia and west Russia—timber, lentils, flax and hemp. Timber is still floated down the streams, and sawn and dressed in the mills at Königsberg. Imports included coal, fertilizers and industrial products, and above all herrings for the Russian market. In the inter-war period imports increased, and were mainly coal and timber, coal coming by water instead of by rail to avoid the crossing of the Polish Corridor. Exports, however, did not reach their pre-1913 level ; they included small quantities of grain, flax, and cellulose, but a third of the ships left in ballast.

The industries of Königsberg occupy about one-third of its inhabitants and commerce another third. The chief of the industries are concerned with the processing of the products of the hinterland of East Prussia, cellulose, paper- and saw-milling, grain-milling, brewing, together with general engineering. The trade of the port reached 3 million tons in 1933. Königsberg, though no great port, is a good example of a regional capital serving a clearly defined political territory, with no competitor to share or reduce its varied functions as an economic and cultural centre. Its famous University was founded in 1544.

Memel became a town in 1252 with Lübeck law and was overlooked by a castle of the Teutonic Order. But its surroundings on the lower Memel were a wilderness of marsh and moor, and the town was essentially a calling station for the Baltic trade. Colonization of the interior did not start till the fifteenth century and the trade of the port was very small. In 1924 Memel was given to Lithuania to serve as a port for this new state. It was seized by the Nazis in 1938 and reunited with East Prussia.

CHAPTER IX

BRANDENBURG—BERLIN

Brandenburg was the nucleus of the modern state of Prussia. It began as a frontier province on the west bank of the lower Elbe—the Altmark, established in the tenth century. Eastward territorial expansion with the conquest of the Slavs carried its frontier to the districts between the Elbe and the Oder in the thirteenth century, and these were grouped together as the Mittelmark, together with Prignitz and Uckermark. This was soon followed by the addition, beyond the Oder, of the Neumark in 1260. The capital cities of the province shifted eastwards, beginning on the lower Elbe with Tangermünde, then shifting to Brandenburg, then to Berlin, while Frankfurt-on-Oder was used as the military base for the conquest of the Neumark. The margravate of Brandenburg was established in 1157 and it became an electorate of the Empire in 1351. The Hohenzollerns came into control in the early fifteenth century and the territories of the march were made indivisible. The real growth of Berlin, however, upon which the present unity of Brandenburg largely depends, began in the seventeenth and eighteenth centuries under the Hohenzollerns, as the capital of Prussia.

Physically, the province corresponds with the zone of wide, flat troughs, stretching from east to west and convex to the south, that are occupied by bends of the main rivers and their tributaries. The heart of the province lies between the Elbe and the Oder, where there are the wide flat lake-strewn valleys of the Havel and the Spree. An island across the latter permitted the siting of two early settlements, Alt Berlin and Kölln, the beginnings of modern Berlin. Marshy floors and sandy tracts of pine forest, like the famous Grünewald, alternate with stretches of higher level land which is more fertile and well cultivated. The centre of the province lies between the Elbe and the Oder with extensions beyond Magdeburg and Frankfurt-on-Oder in the Altmark and the Neumark, the central section being known as the Mittelmark. The province is limited by the wide valley to the north that is occupied in turn by the lower Elbe, the lowest bend of the Oder, the Warthe-Netze valley, and the lowest bend of the Vistula. Beyond this valley, to the north, lie the Baltic Uplands. To the south it is limited by the Fläming Heath, a wide belt of uplands, with heath and wood and patches of cultivation, which until recently was very thinly peopled.   Between these limits the territory of Brandenburg expanded eastwards from the Altmark.   The more fertile soils on the better-drained lands were first occupied—this fact probably accounting for the early extension of the fertile prong of the Uckermark towards Stettin.   The marshy and forested areas are still largely in their natural condition, although, especially under Frederick the Great, considerable areas were drained, cultivated, and settled.   Here, too, were built the canals that, in the shape of a cross, centre on Berlin, and link the Havel and the Spree with the Elbe and the Oder.

Agriculturally, Brandenburg is a province of poor sandy soils. Over a third of its total area is under forest, and it has a markedly lower proportion of farmed land than the fertile Baltic provinces to the north and the *Börde* zone to the south of it.   It also stands in contrast to these in respect of its farming, for nearly a fifth of the arable land is under potatoes, holdings are small or medium in size (21 to 50 hectares), and the number of its agricultural workers per unit of land is the lowest in Germany.   Moor and meadow cover its extensive flat, marshy, valley floors, especially in the Havelland, while arable land accounts for about a third to two-fifths of the area.   On the cultivated land, the sandy soils carry rye, oats and potatoes ; wheat and barley are grown on the better soils, and there is a marked concentration of more intensive market gardening near the capital.   Cattle raising is also of considerable importance and especially dairy farming near the capital for the sale of fluid milk.   Associated with rye and potato production, as elsewhere in Germany, there is a large output of pigs.   There are scattered deposits of brown coal, but these are dwarfed into insignificance by the great production of Lower Lusatia.

Industries began as handicrafts in the small country towns. The old manufacture of textiles, formerly concentrated in Berlin, shifted to surrounding towns in the nineteenth century, and is now concentrated on the brown-coalfield of Lower Lusatia.   The engineering industries owed their modern development to the stimulus of the kings of Prussia in the early eighteenth century, who had erected arms plants at Potsdam and Spandau (1722) and caused the introduction of the manufacture of cutlery at Neustadt-Eberswalde (1743).   Light engineering industries have persisted to this day in the small towns ; the manufacture of bicycles is a notable new addition.   The glass industry, the greatest industry of Brandenburg after textiles, located on the

Lusatian brown-coalfield, dates from the end of the eighteenth century.

Railways radiate throughout the province from Berlin. Especially remarkable in the growth of Berlin are the waterways. Lying midway between the Elbe and the Oder on the waterways and lakes of the Havel and the Spree, Berlin is at a natural crossways of navigable waterways which have been supplemented by canal connections. The Plauer canal joins the Elbe with the Havel ; the Havelland canal connects Berlin and the lower Havel ; the Oder-Spree canal joins Berlin southeastwards with the Oder at Fürstenberg ; the Teltow canal skirts the south of Berlin in making its way to Potsdam. Especially important is the ship canal from Berlin to the Oder and thence to Stettin.

Greater Berlin gives real unity to the modern province of Brandenburg. Greater Berlin was formed in 1920 by the combination of old Berlin with ninety-three surrounding parishes and towns. The total area of this new district is 341 square miles and it had a population in 1939 of just over 4¼ millions. About 46 per cent. of the population depend on industry, 28 per cent. on commerce and transport, 8 per cent. on administration, 7 per cent. on social service, etc., and the rest are without paid occupation. The proportion dependent on industry is not very high (compare Saxony, 56 per cent., Westphalia, 57 per cent.), but the numbers engaged in commerce and transport and administration are more than double the average for the Reich and indicate the pre-eminence of Berlin as the capital of the Reich. Moreover, the industries are typical of those of every great city. The chief are the production of electrical apparatus, engineering and clothing, followed by the building trades, foods and printing and publishing. Two-fifths of all its workers are engaged in the finished steel and metal industries, the chief being the production of electrical apparatus, of which it is the main centre of production in Germany.

Berlin, like all great cities, imports great quantities of bulky materials—mainly foodstuffs and building materials and fuels—and exports relatively small quantities of manufactured goods in small consignments by rail. The total traffic in and out by rail and water amounts to about 30 million tons per year. Eighty per cent. is inward traffic, two-thirds going by rail and one-third by water, and 20 per cent. is outward traffic, four-fifths going by rail and one-fifth by water. The inward traffic consists of coal,

briquettes, building materials and grain. The outward traffic
includes iron and steel goods, fertilizers and chemicals. Berlin
is the greatest railway centre in Germany, and is one of its great
inland river ports, its traffic being distributed among nine river
harbours, the chief being the Westhafen and the Osthafen, both
in the city.

The build of Berlin is such that its nucleus is the old town
centre of Berlin and Kölln and the court district of Dorotheen-
stadt and Friedrichsstadt founded in the early eighteenth century.
The whole of this nucleus to-day forms the greater part of the
central business district, with the headquarters of business,
shopping, culture, and administration. Around this cluster of
specialized districts, there is a sea of closely packed tenements
and factories with large expanses of railway yards adjacent to
the stations, public buildings, etc., and this whole area, housing
over a half of the total population of Greater Berlin ($2\frac{1}{4}$ million),
is encircled by a clearly defined circular railway known as the
Ringbahn. Since 1880 the new industrial plants—mainly electrical and general engineering—have been established outside
this circular railway and have expanded outwards along the
railways and waterways well beyond the limits of the present
administrative area of Greater Berlin.[1] Greater Berlin, with its
industrial axis on the north-west to south-east line of the Havel-
Spree, reaches out to the old towns of Spandau and Potsdam
in the west and Köpenik in the south-east.

It is significant that the whole of Greater Berlin is accessible to the main traffic centres of the city—Alexanderplatz and
Wittenbergplatz—within an hour, and that there are extensions
also accessible in this time along the main railway routes for
about 10 kilometres beyond the city limits—beyond Spandau
and Potsdam in the west, Wildau and Erkner in the east,
Bernau in the north-east, and Velten and Oranienburg in the
north. These outlying places, and several still farther afield
within a distance of 50 kilometres, have industries that fall within
the sphere of the labour market of Berlin—that is, that are
accessible for workers living in Berlin, and that also are largely
directed from Berlin. The upper Havel valley to the north-west,
alongside the Stettin canal, includes Henningsdorf, Velten and
Oranienburg, and has electrical supply plants, steel and rolling

[1] The chief of these industrial areas, inside Greater Berlin, but on the outskirts
of the built-up area, are Spandau-Siemenstadt in the west ; Tegel-Wittenau-
Reinickendorf in the north, clustered on the Tegel lake ; and Schöneweide along
the Spree and reaching to Köpenik in the south-east.

mills, and chemical works. Potsdam to the south-west and the small places of Nowawes and Teltow, lying to the south-west alongside the main railway to Berlin and the Teltow canal, have miscellaneous light industries. Eberswalde, farther afield to the north-east alongside the Stettin canal, also has miscellaneous industries, including engineering. These industries are obviously tied up closely with the water and railway routes radiating from Berlin.

The broad economic structure of the Berlin-Brandenburg region has been outlined by a German writer on the planning problems of Berlin and Brandenburg as follows. At distances over 100 kilometres from Berlin there are smaller cities that are independent trade and cultural centres—Dresden, Leipzig, Halle, Stettin and Magdeburg. Nearer to Berlin, and actually near the political frontiers of the province of Brandenburg, about 100 kilometres distant from Berlin, are medium-sized towns that serve in large measure as independent centres, though these are already dependent in some ways on Berlin. The 80-to-100 kilometres radius passes through the Elbe to the west (beyond the town of Brandenburg at the western end of the Havel lowland), and the Oder to the east with Frankfurt at the end of the Spree route. To the north it passes along the Finow and Stettin canals along which there is no old-standing town centre. To the south it passes through Jüterborg to the south-west and Lübben to the south-east, which mark roughly the beginning of the uplands of the Fläming and Lower Lusatian heathlands. These towns are independent trade centres with independent industries and labour markets. The towns of Lower Lusatia, such as Kottbus, Forst and Güben to the south of Berlin, owe their important textile industries to migration from Berlin and they supply the Berlin clothing industry; but they also have a nation-wide market and form a separate economic unit. The brown-coal field supplies briquettes and electricity to Berlin, and is thus closely allied with the Berlin-Brandenburg complex; it also lies inside the political province of Brandenburg. To the south-west, along and beyond the Elbe, none of the many small towns has been able to reach a large size. This is true, for instance, of Zerbst and Wittenberg on the Elbe. All these towns are closely related to the economic complex of the central German brown-coalfield. Dessau, the capital of Anhalt with important aircraft industries, has grown rapidly in the last twenty years. Wittenberg, 90 kilometres from Berlin, is a historic bridgehead about half-way between Berlin and Leipzig. Though closely allied culturally with Central Germany in the Middle Ages, and having its own ancient University, it owes its modern industrial development to the Berlin market. Together with Brandenburg and Frankfurt these towns have had a large measure of independent economic development, based on local natural resources. They also supply their local agricultural markets, and they draw mainly upon local labour supplies for their industries.

Still nearer Berlin, between 80 and 40 kilometres radius, the towns are smaller than those farther afield and are directly associated with the economic sphere of Berlin. Industries are linked, in both the supply of their products and the marketing of their materials, with Berlin firms and their trade and business are concentrated in Berlin. This zone is, in general, very thinly peopled, with extensive areas of forest to the east and west, and considerable areas of cultivated land to the north and south but with no towns of any significance. It is dominated by Berlin, however, serving as a " week-end area " for summer outings, and has outlying high-class suburban districts (*Trabantenstädte*). Its rural economy—market-gardening, dairying, etc.—is oriented to the Berlin market.

Towns distant 30 to 20 kilometres from the centre of Berlin lie at the ends of the Berlin suburban railway net and are accessible to the centre just within the hour, as noticed above. They therefore lie within the range of the Berlin labour market and are intimately tied up with the social and economic sphere of the city of Berlin. If the circular railway (*Ringbahn*) be regarded as a circle with a radius of about 5 kilometres, then this zone lies outside it, within 25 to 15 kilometres of the centre of Berlin. It includes all the major industrial areas of Greater Berlin and the areas of recent residential development, settled since about 1880 with the extension of urban development beyond the *Ringbahn*.

This concentric belting of zones around a great city nucleus, which is a normal development in the growth and expansion of all cities, is particularly well marked in Berlin and serves as a good example of the general arrangement of the zones of influence of a great city. It illustrates the case for the expansion of the political limits of a city so as to include the outlying areas that in the last fifty years have become virtually a part of it through the expansion of houses, factories and communications and the whole fabric of space relations that depends on the mobility these things imply. It also demonstrates the way in which smaller towns are grouped around the main city and how, nearer the latter, town growth is stifled, while, farther away from it, small towns of very early origin, contemporaneous with the capital city, lag behind in their modern growth and divide their allegiance between two or more great cities, and are in themselves in large measure independent economic and cultural centres. It illustrates also the process whereby, during the nineteenth century, industries in the city centre shifted gradually to the towns in its environs and, indeed, over a wide surrounding area. This has been especially true of the textile and heavier engineering industries. Lastly, it illustrates how a relatively isolated backward area—Lower Lusatia—in its rapid modern economic development has become markedly oriented to the capital, supplying it with vital needs—power and fuel— although itself, through the development of specialized industries, having nation-wide and independent connections.

The relations of Berlin with its region have, of course, close similarities with the relations of London—the " city ", the county of London, Greater London and the Home Counties ; and Paris—the city, the area inside the nineteenth-century fortifications, the limits of Greater Paris reaching to the boundaries of the Department of the Seine, and further still the area closely allied to Paris that has been defined for purposes of " regional planning " as a radius of 35 kilometres from the city centre.

Each city and its environs has its peculiar features, but the general zonal arrangements based on space relations centred on the city nucleus are the same. Economic orientation towards Berlin, coupled with the distinctive characteristics of the land and its farming, give to Brandenburg its unity.

CHAPTER X

SILESIA

I

The Prussian Province of Silesia was conquered and annexed by Frederick the Great in 1742. Originally Polish and with a population almost entirely Polish in Upper Silesia until the eighteenth century, it passed from Poland to the kingdom of Bohemia in 1526 and was absorbed into the Habsburg dominions until its conquest by Prussia. At that time, the more closely settled section was in the centre, around Breslau, while the northern area (Lower Silesia) was thinly-peopled heathland, and the southern area in Upper Silesia was also forested with a scattered Polish-speaking population. The central area, together with the Sudetes uplands, is thus the historic core of Silesia with its capital in Breslau. But the southern sector has one of the greatest coalfields in Europe, and its development in the last two generations as a new, populous, industrial orbit of human organization and space-relations has created one of the thorniest problems of political geography in central Europe.

The political unit of Silesia, embracing the three strongly contrasted sectors noted above, has nevertheless been a permanent politico-geographical unit for centuries. It has its nucleus in a great bay of lowland that is drained northwards by the Oder river, and before 1919 reached for centuries as far as the Vistula above Cracow. This lowland on the west side of the Oder to the foot of the Sudetes uplands is open, treeless, black-earth land and is extremely fertile.[1] It is to-day one of the greatest agricultural areas in Germany, producing large quantities of sugar-beet and wheat, as in the *Börde* zone farther west. This area is encircled by poorer and, in general, forested upland country. The forest lowland of Upper Silesia is enclosed by uplands, with lowland breaks leading through to the Vistula basin (Cracow) and through the Moravian Gate to the March valley and through to Brno and Vienna. The Sudetes uplands to the west, where lies the frontier against Bohemia (Czechoslovakia), like all the upland blocks of the Central Uplands, is rolling upland country, with some more rugged mountainous areas, like the famous Riesengebirge. It is mainly forested, with large tracts of land

---

[1] Middle Silesia has over two-thirds of its total area under arable land.

cleared for cultivation in the Middle Ages in its broad valley floors and enclosed depressions. It is poor farming land with small holdings, and has long been a seat of mining and in later centuries of the textile and other industries. The edge of the Polish uplands to the east is also an infertile wooded country with the same poor farming conditions (rye and potatoes), but with relatively little industrial development except in the towns. A zone of low hills, covered with woods and heath to the north, stretches from south-east to north-west from central Poland through Lusatia to the Fläming and Lüneburg Heaths. At the northern end of the Sudetes uplands in Upper Lusatia, grew a series of not unimportant medieval towns on the great east–west routeway from Leipzig to Breslau. Moreover, under the Prussian kings, in the eighteenth century the development of the textile industries, as in Saxony, was encouraged in the Sudetes uplands, and this was again fostered in the nineteenth century by the mining of coal in lowland pockets in the uplands, the chief of which is centred on Waldenburg. In 1815 the Sudetes uplands was the most populous region in Silesia. The emergence of an entirely new industrial complex in Upper Silesia and of the brown-coal industrial area in Lower Silesia and Lusatia in the northern heathlands during the last seventy years has upset the equilibrium of this ancient historical unit.

Particularly interesting is the way in which Lower and Upper Lusatia to the north have so often changed their political allegiance, for historically they have been more or less independent units. The latter is centred on the series of medieval towns noted above (p. 131) that combined to form the Six Towns League. The former was a thinly-peopled and poverty-stricken border zone until the advent of brown-coal attracted modern glass, chemical and textile industries, developed in part from earlier beginnings based on local charcoal. The allegiance of both units has been divided in history between Saxony, Brandenburg (Prussia) and Bohemia. They have normally been outside the Silesian province and formed part of the Saxon kingdom with the frontier running so as to bring the Bober valley (flowing from south to north) into Silesia. It was not until 1815 that Lower Lusatia was added to Brandenburg, and since then its economic development has been dominantly associated with Berlin and Brandenburg, rather than southwards, although its brown-coal mining and its associated industries give to the area much in common with Central Germany west of the Elbe. This is a first-class instance of an

area, formerly thinly peopled and a border zone, being transformed by modern industrial development and having close
connections, in the present as in the past, with several—in this
case three—regional orbits.

The development of the coalfield in Upper Silesia has, of
course, completely upset the historic equilibrium of this extreme
corner of Germany that borders on Poland and Czechoslovakia
and their predecessors, Russia and the Habsburg dominions of
Austria. The pre-1918 frontier was one of the most clear-cut
divides of political, cultural and economic associations in Europe,
a fact due not only to the differences between the character of
the German and Russian governments and the German and
Polish people living on either side of it, but also to the deliberate
policy of Russia to cut relationships across the Prussian frontier
from the Carpathians to the Baltic to a minimum. During
this period virtually the whole of the developed coalfield, and
indeed most of the coalfield, lay inside the boundaries of the
Reich, as founded in 1871. The division of the field was a
necessity for the national existence of Poland and Czechoslovakia. The allocation of Polish and German areas was based
on a plebiscite, though this was complicated by the fact that
Polish workers in the towns had adopted German speech and
ways. The definition of the new boundary was extremely difficult, for national and economic conditions had to be catered for
by cutting the boundary right through the populous industrial
area, so that the bulk of it passed to Poland, leaving the industrial
triangle of Beuthen, Gleiwitz and Hindenburg to Germany. The
new boundary as defined in 1923 " surely crosses more lines of
transportation than any other equal stretch of international
boundary in the world ", writes an unbiased American scholar,
and it severs the unity of a single industrial and population unit.
Special arrangements were made by the League of Nations to
permit free intercourse across the frontier, but these expired in
1937 and the whole question was seriously aggravated by the
attitude of the Nazi authorities to the Polish folk in German
territory and the Germans on the Polish side in the dark days
of the industrial depression in the 'thirties. Almost the entire
area belonged to Germany before the last war, and had a
single net of narrow-gauge freight lines, electric tramways, a
single power system and water supply, though there has naturally been much reorientation during the subsequent period.
The total area of the coalfield is about 5,500 square kilometres,

and 4,000 square kilometres belong to Poland. The total production of coal amounts to about 70 million tons—20 million in the German section, 10 million in the Czech section and 35 to 40 million in the Polish section. Almost all the zinc- and lead-producing area is in Polish territory.

The inter-war period has shown, and the future of this area will reveal even more clearly—for this is the greatest field in Europe after the Ruhr and the Donetz, and is still in the beginnings of its development—that such a complex, though it may be divided politically, must function as a unit in the organization of its industry, its public services, the movements of its population, and the organization of its labour market, especially as such unified development took place in the fifty years before the new boundaries split it up after the last war. This is essential, quite apart from the necessity for freedom of movement of its products, especially coal to markets, unhindered by tariff restrictions, and for the development of improved transport facilities to the Vistula, the Oder and the Danube. A new canal connection has recently been opened on the German side to link up with the Oder at Kosel, and the Poles have built new railways and a new port—Gdynia—to serve as an outlet for the surplus coal to the Scandinavian market. Moreover, the future markets of the coal and the iron and steel and other products of the area lie in east central Europe, not in Germany, where Silesian coal now has to meet the competition of Ruhr coal and the brown-coal briquettes and electric power of central Germany and Lusatia. Austria, Czechoslovakia and Poland all require coal in connection with their iron and steel industries and other industrial and domestic needs, and each of these countries (especially Austria) has surplus iron-ore reserves, while there will be an ever-increasing market in south-eastern Europe for its heavy iron and steel products. The markets of Upper Silesia lie in east-central Europe rather than in Germany, and freedom of exchange with these countries is necessary to its future prosperity.

II

It will be of interest to discuss at a little greater length the industrial development of Silesia.

At the end of the eighteenth century the Sudetes upland was the most important textile manufacturing district in Germany, especially for linen goods. This was a cottage industry, and was

encouraged by various royal favours. With the tardy introduction of machinery in the 'forties, a gradual change took place
from linen to cotton weaving in factories in towns, the cottage
industry dying out almost completely. The textile industries
have remained in the same districts in the Sudetes (linen and
damasks), Lower Silesia, with centres at Reichenbach, Lauban
and Landeshut (cotton, with linen as a subsidiary), and in
Saxony (cotton). The woollen industry is markedly concentrated in a few towns—Forst, Güben, and Kottbus, in northern
Silesia and Lower Lusatia and southern Brandenburg. Coal
supplies are available nearby for steam power from Upper
Silesia and Waldenburg in the Sudetes. But the growth, survival and modern importance of the textile industries is due
above all to the large skilled labour supply, in poor farming
country, from which, on their small holdings, the folk are unable
to eke out a living. Two other industries in the uplands, that
grew out of the readjustments in the mid-nineteenth century
and have undergone various changes in production and organization with changing conditions, are wood-working, especially
match-making, and paper-making in the Riesengebirge, using
local timber, running water, and rags from the linen industry.
The latter, still using local paper and pulp and coal, is still closely
tied to the rivers especially along the Oder from Ratibor to
Maltsch. Here there are paper, pulp and cellulose mills and
factories.

The mining and smelting of metals began soon after the
German settlement in the Middle Ages. They occurred only at
scattered points in the Sudetes, but became of chief importance
in Lower Lusatia and Upper Silesia, using low-grade ores and
timber (for charcoal). The iron industry is recorded in the
former as far back as the thirteenth century, though pits and
smelteries were shifted from place to place.[1] Not till the
fifteenth and sixteenth centuries, with the use of running water
for working the forges, did the industry become fixed to definite
sites along the many streams that cross the heathland. Blast
furnaces, using charcoal as fuel, were not introduced until the
eighteenth century.

In Upper Silesia, the oldest mining and smelting district was
around Tarnowitz and Beuthen (see Fig. 29), where the mining

[1] Local and widespread brown (or bog) iron ores (*Raseneizenerze*) were used. As
these are quickly renewed by natural processes, it was possible to return after
a period to the same places and find new deposits. In other words, at this stage
it was a shifting industry.

of silver and lead began in the early sixteenth century, and coal-
mining in the eighteenth century ; but this was all very unimportant.   After the conquest of Silesia, Frederick the Great
caused the foundation of an iron and steel industry to supply his
army with munitions, and this was sited not in these older districts
but in the forest near Malapane and Kreuzburg.   It used charcoal and the low-grade surface ores, and the labour was drawn

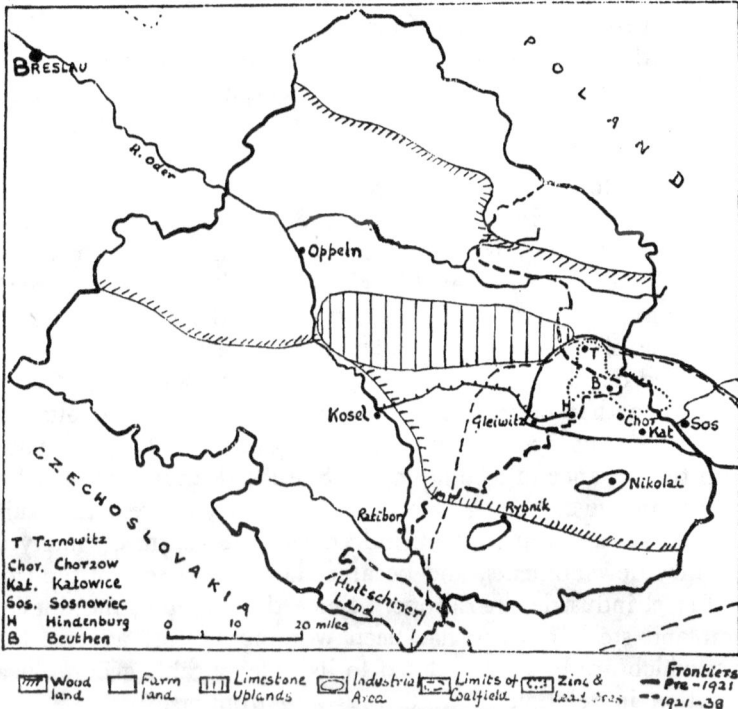

FIG. 29.—Upper Silesia.
Types of Country and Location of Industrial Area in relation to the frontiers.

from Saxony and the Harz, both the traditional metal-working
districts.   By 1780 there were thirty-six furnaces.   Higher grade
iron ores were also discovered at this time in the old Tarnowitz
district.

Coal was later available as a fuel for the furnace.   It began
to be obtained from surface workings about 1750, and with the
increasing demand for coal for iron smelting, the latter shifted
southwards to the coal-mines, the northern district still surviving
by using the local ores and charcoal.   In 1796 the first coked

G

blast furnace in Europe was opened at Gleiwitz. Railways and
the building of a canal to the Oder added to its importance, and
in 1850 it was the biggest iron producer in Germany, yielding
about 40 per cent. of the total. After this date it suffered from
the competition of the Ruhr, which was much more favourably
situated geographically, near to the river Rhine. Moreover, the
Silesian ores were too poor in grade and small in quantity to
meet the demands of the growing industry, and ores had to be
imported from Styria and Hungary. In the last decades of the
nineteenth century the Siemens-Martin furnace for steel-making
gradually took the place of the old " puddling " process, and this
furnace consumes scrap-iron together with iron ore. But Upper
Silesia was again badly placed in respect of supplies of scrap-iron,
which had to be drawn over very long distances. Though not
at first a serious disadvantage (since far more coal was used than
ore in the smelting), with the improvement in smelting methods,
less coal was needed to smelt a given quantity of ore—a general
process in the history of the industry—and the Silesian coalfield
lost some of its power of attraction for the industry. Finally,
an added disadvantage was that the coal was not well suited for
coking, so that better-grade coke had to be imported and the
local coke kept for other purposes such as household use. Thus,
with the advance in technique, the Silesian district gradually lost
the advantage of having its own fuel and ore, whereas the Ruhr
was able to keep abreast of, indeed was the centre of, many of
the new developments, and became the greatest seat of the iron
and steel industries in Europe. Since the 'nineties, the Silesian
iron and steel industry has been working against adverse factors which are basically related to its unfavourable geographical
situation in relation to waterways and frontiers.

The zinc industry also developed in the Silesian area. The
calamine deposits were first used for making brass, though they
were not suited for the production of raw zinc. The smelting
of zinc dated from 1798 in the forest of Wessola. But the new
industry developed on the coalfield like the iron industry. For
a time Silesia dominated the world zinc market, but when it was
discovered, in the 'seventies, that zinc could be smelted from
zinc blende new seats of production sprang up, especially in the
United States, and Silesia lost its world pre-eminence, though it
retained the ever-increasing home market.

All this development proceeded almost entirely in German
territory before 1914. By the Treaty of Versailles, the area

passed mainly to Poland. Germany lost 75 per cent. of the coal production, two-thirds of the pig-iron capacity, all the iron ore, and 85 per cent. of the zinc and lead production. Virtually all the ores are now imported to the German sector from Sweden. Only 15 per cent. of the coke is used in furnaces. Projects have been made to shift the German iron and steel industry to more favourable sites, especially to the Oder between Breslau and Maltsch, where ores could be brought through Stettin up the Oder direct to the plant, and coke could be brought from Waldenburg. No such shift has in fact taken place. Indeed, the conquest of the whole Polish and Czech area by the Nazis and its complete absorption into the war economy of the Reich has given a great fillip to production throughout the area. The survival of the German Silesian heavy industry is only possible by State financial support, for there is need for the canalizing of the Oder (a new canal from Kosel taking 450-ton barges has recently been opened), and the Silesian products certainly require preferential tariff treatment on the German railways, in order to compete in eastern Germany with those of the Ruhr. The situation is made even more unfavourable to Silesia by the completion of the Mittelland canal that permits Ruhr coal to reach Berlin and beyond.

The fate of the Polish section of the field in the inter-war period has been more serious than the German, through the breaking of contact with the German market (which before the last war took 40 per cent. of the coal, 65 per cent. of the iron and steel and 90 per cent. of the zinc), and the lack of transport facilities by rail and water on the Polish side, and the inadequacy of the Polish market to absorb its output of coal. A new railway was built by the Polish government to Gdynia to serve as the outlet for coal destined for Scandinavia, though apparently, through specially reduced tariff rates, this has been run at a loss to the Polish State.

Lower Silesia also has its coalfield at Waldenburg, situated in a saucer-shaped depression in the Sudetes uplands west of Breslau. Mining began on a considerable scale in the second half of the nineteenth century, but did not really flourish until the advent of the railway. It gives a good coking coal that is used in the Silesian textile factories. There are no heavy industries, except for porcelain making, on the field, which is small in area and lacking in suitable sites.

The low, heath-covered uplands of Lower Silesia and Lower

Lusatia had an old-established iron industry that died hard with its old methods. Most of the charcoal-burning furnaces had ceased to function in the 'seventies, the last closing down in 1900. But the old smelters survive as foundries and enamel works, using Waldenburg coke and pig-iron from the Ruhr. This area is to-day dominated by the two new industries of glass and brown-coal. The glass industry is very ancient in Silesia in both the Sudetes uplands and in the lowland heaths. Like the early iron smelting, it was closely tied to its raw materials, sand and charcoal, and at first was shifted from site to site. Fixation came in the seventeenth century with the establishment of glass smelters (most of the workers hailing from Bohemia), especially in the valleys where running water could be used. The chief districts became the Glatz uplands, Riesengebirge and Hirschberg, where the industry is still located, producing high-quality goods, though it is subordinate to textiles. The dominance of glass-making in Lower Lusatia is based on the occurrence of brown-coal deposits, whose exploitation began in the 'forties. But this was of no use as a fuel for producing high temperatures until after the advent of the briquetting process at the end of the century. Then, both brown-coal and glass production forged ahead. Brown-coal supplied not only the glass industry, but also brick-making and ceramics (through the occurrence together of brown-coal and clay). Aluminium smelting was also introduced during the last war and great electric power plants were established.

III

Silesia figures regularly as a unit in nation-wide divisions, with occasionally a division into Upper and Lower Silesia, the former being grouped around the coalfield. This division is found, for instance, in the new arrangement of the Nazi Party districts, Upper Silesia including the whole of the coalfield area, German and Polish.[1]

Breslau is the historic and modern capital of Silesia. It is the main railroad centre and the dominant collecting and distributing centre. In 1933 the numbers engaged in the two large

[1] The Prussian Province of Silesia has been extended since the outbreak of war to include all the Upper Silesian industrial area, including Teschen and the frontier carried into south-west Poland beyond the 1914 frontier. Thus, it is important to note carefully, this area is incorporated by the Nazis into the Reich and its organization. This new province assuming its historic outline falls into two Nazi *Gaue*, Upper and Lower Silesia.

groups of industry and of commerce were the same ; moreover,
since 1907 there has been a decrease in industrial employment (due probably in the main to the depression in the early
'thirties), but a large increase in commercial employment.
Industries are mixed and there is no dominant group. They
are evidently concerned in very large measure with catering for
this extensive regional market, for which, as a great prolongation
of German territory to the south-east, Breslau, on the main lines
to Upper Silesia, occupies a dominating geographical position.
Clothing occupies 12·7 per cent. of its workers, engineering
8·3 per cent., food and drink 8·2 per cent., and the building
trades 7·3 per cent.

That Breslau's economy has primarily a regional orientation
is revealed by rail and water traffic statistics.[1]

RAILWAY AND WATER TRAFFIC OF BRESLAU IN 1932 IN TONS

	Railway.		Waterway (Oder).	
	Despatch.	Receipt.	Despatch.	Receipt.
Upper Silesia . .	101,000	826,000	20,000	19,000
Lower Silesia . .	271,000	761,000	7,000	500
Reich	94,000	238,000	308,000	233,000

Receipts from Lower Silesia were mainly foodstuffs, stones and
earths, and coal. From Upper Silesia coal dwarfed all other
products. The dispatches are, as for all big cities, much smaller
in bulk than the receipts. They are very varied and evenly
balanced. Metal wares, machinery, foods, are outstanding.
Nearly all this traffic is effected by rail. But, on the other hand,
exports to and imports from other parts of the Reich by river
are high, indicating the importance of the city as a break-of-
bulk point—only third in importance on the Oder after Stettin
at the mouth and Kosel at the head of navigation. The majority
of Breslau's traffic with the Reich by rail and water is with
Saxony, Brandenburg and Berlin.

Thus, in conclusion, while Silesia, until the cession of the
Upper Silesian areas in 1919, has been a permanent political
unit for centuries, there was a marked geographical diversity
within it, even before the development of the coalfield added a
further complicating element. Before the development of the

[1] From Paul Driske, *Der Wirtschaftsorganismus Gross-Breslau*, pp. 147–62.

coalfield, it is true to say that the most populous and industrialized districts, of no mean importance at that time, lay in the Sudetes uplands in Silesia and their continuation in Upper Lusatia and Saxony and across the Bohemian border. The most fertile lands lie between the Oder and the Sudetes, while agriculturally poor lands lie on the heaths and woods to the east of the Oder and to the north across the province. Breslau is the dominant historic and modern focus, but the growth of modern industry in Upper Silesia and Lower Silesia and Lower Lusatia has caused some measure of reorientation and decentralization in its regional association. In the case of Upper Silesia, this has given rise to problems affecting not only Silesia, but also the vital economic interests of east-central Europe.

BIBLIOGRAPHY

PERIODICALS

Many articles on the subject of regional reconstruction in general and on the structure and problems of particular regions have appeared in the following periodicals :
Zeitschrift für Geopolitik.
Erde und Wirtschaft. (1927, ceased publication 1934.) .
Deutsche Zeitschrift für Wirtschaftskunde. (Commenced publication 1936.)
Raumforschung und Raumordnung, monthly journal of the *Reichsarbeitsgemeinschaft für Raumforschung.* (Commenced publication 1936.)

CHAPTER I : REGIONALISM IN GERMANY

.W. Vogel. *Deutschlands bundesstaatliche Neugestaltung,* Berlin, 1919.
—— *Deutsche Reichsgliederung und Reichsreform in Vergangenheit und Gegenwart,* Teubner, Berlin, 1932. Contains short bibliography of works on the constitutional, historical and geographical aspects.
E. Obst, *Zur Neugliederung des Deutschen Reiches, Zeit. f. Geopolitik,* Heft 5, 1928.
A. Weitzel, *Die regionale Gliederung Deutschlands nach Wirtschafts- und Verkehrsgebieten, Erde und Wirtschaft,* Heft 2, 1928–9.
—— and Schrepfer, H. *Deutschlands Neugliederung nach dem " Frankfurter Entwurf ",* Frankfurt-am-M., 1931.

CHAPTER II : GERMANY AS A WHOLE

E. Tiessen. *Deutscher Wirtschaftsatlas* (Reichsverband der Deutschen Industrie, Berlin, 1929).
E. Scheu. *Deutschlands Wirtschaftsgeographische Harmonie,* Breslau, 1924.
—— *Des Reiches wirtschaftliche Einheit,* Berlin, 1926.
—— *Die wirtschaftsgeographische Gliederung Deutschlands, Erde und Wirtschaft,* Band I, 1927–8.
—— *Deutschlands Wirtschaftsprovinzen und Wirtschaftsbezirke, Weltpolitische Bücherei, Länderkundliche Reihe,* Band 2, Berlin, 1928.
W. Volz. *Die Wirtschaftsgeographische Struktur des Deutschen Reiches,* Wissenschaftlichen Veröffentlichungen des Deutschen Museums zu Leipzig, 1936.
J. Müller. *Wirtschaftskunde von Deutschland auf wirtschaftsgeographische u. Wirtschaftsgeschichtliche Grundlage,* Leipzig, 1936.
H. Baumann. *Kraftquellen und Verkehr als Bestimmende Faktoren für deutsche Wirtschaftsgebiete, Verkehrstechnische Woche,* 1923 (3 articles).
W. Christhaller. *Die Zentralen Orte Süddeutschlands,* Jena, 1933.
G. v. Geldern-Crispendorf. *Die Deutschen Industriegebiete, ihre Entstehung und Entwicklung, Deutsche Sammlung, Reihe Geographie,* Band 4, Karlsruhe, 1933.
M. Pfannschmidt. *Standort, Landesplanung, Baupolitik,* Berlin, 1932.
H. Ende. *Die Verkehrsdichte des Deutschen Reiches, Archiv f. Eisenbahnwesen,* Hefte 3–4, 1936.
O. Schlier. *Die Landschaften Deutschlands,* Allgemeine Statistisches Archiven, Band 20, 1930.

167

P. Schulz-Kresow. " Gütertarifpolitik und Raumordnung ", *Raumforschung und Raumordnung*, Heft 3, 1936.
——— " Ballungstendenzen der Verkehrsnetze ", with four maps, *Raumforschung und Raumordnung*, Heft 4, 1937.
W. Tuckermann. "Vorschläge für eine Neugliederung des Deutschen Reiches ", in B. Schmittmann, *Preussen-Deutschland oder deutsches Deutschland*, Bonn, 1920.
F. Zahn. *Die raumwirtschaftliche Verflechtung der deutschen Volkswirtschaft, Erde und Wirtschaft*, Heft 1, 1927.
E. De Martonne. *Europe Centrale*, 2 vols., Géographie Universelle, 1929.

CHAPTER III : RHINELAND-WESTPHALIA

H. Aubin, O. Bühler, B. Kuske and A. Schulte. *Der Raum Westfalen*, vol. I, *Grundlagen und Zusammenhänge*, Berlin, 1931.
O. Most, B. Kuske and H. Weber. *Wirtschaftskunde für Rheinland und Westfalen*, Berlin, 1931. Two volumes, standard work.
H. Spethmann. *Ruhrrevier und Raum Westfalen, Wirtschaftskritische Ergänzung zu dem Werk " Der Raum Westfalen "*, Oldenburg, 1933.
B. Kuske. *Die Groszstadt Köln als wirtschaftlicher und Sozialer Körper*, Köln, 1928.
——— *Die Volkswirtschaft des Rheinlandes in ihrer Eigenart und Bedeutung*, Essen, 1925.

CHAPTER IV : LOWER SAXONY

K. Brüning. *Niedersachsen im Rahmen der Neugliederung des Reiches, Veröff. d. Wirtschaftswiss. Ges. z. Stud. Niedersachsens*, Band I, 1929, Band II, 1931, Hanover.
W. Pessler. *Der Niedersächsische Kulturkreis*, Hanover, 1925.
E. Obst. *Niedersachsen und das Reich, Veröff. der Wirtschaftswissenschaftlichen Gesellschaft zum Studium Niedersachsen*, Hanover, 1925.

CHAPTER V : HANSA CITIES, HAMBURG AND BREMEN

G. Kappe. *Die Unterweser und ihr Wirtschaftsraum*, 1929.
R. Lütgens. *Die deutschen Seehäfen, Deutsche Sammlung, Reihe Geographie*, Band 6, Karlsruhe, 1934.
F. Schumacher. *Das Gebiet Unterelbe-Hamburg im Rahmen einer Neugliederung des Reiches*, Hamburg, 1932.
R. Lütgens. " Hansestadt Hamburg ", *Geographische Zeitschrift*, XLIII, 1937, deals with the territorial changes effected by the Nazi law of Jan. 26, 1937. See also W. Vogel in *Petermanns Mitteilungen*, 1937, pp. 65–6.
W. Thalenhorst. *Bremen im Rahmen der Neugliederung des Reiches*, Bremen, 1932.

CHAPTER VI : SOUTHERN GERMANY

R. Reinhard and K. Voppel. *Land und Volk an der Saar*, Museum f. Länderkunde zu Leipzig, 1934.
Capot-Rey. *La Région Industrielle Sarroise, Territoire de la Sarre et bassin houiller de la Moselle, Étude Géographique*, Paris, 1934.
W. Ehmer. *Südwestdeutschland als Einheit und Wirtschaftsraum*, Stuttgart, 1930.
H. Losch. " Die Statistik der Pendelwanderung ", *Württembergische Jahrbücher f. Statistik und Landeskunde*, 1929.
C. Lüer. *Das Rhein-Main Gebiet als wirtschafts- und verkehrsgeographische Einheit*, Deutsche Zeit. für Wirtschaftskunde, Heft 1, 1936.

H. Schrepfer. *Über Wirtschaftsgebiete und ihre Bedeutung für die Wirtschafts-geographie, mit besonderer Berücksichtigung des Rhein-Mainischen Raumes*, Geographische Wochenschrift, 1935, pp. 497–520.
E. Heiligenthal. *Landesplanung im Oberrheingebiet*, Heidelberg, 1934.
R. Kluss. *Bahnwanderung der pfälzischen Arbeiter zwischen Wohnort und Arbeitsort*, Beiträge zur Statistik Bayerns, Heft 93, 1920.
J. H. Schulze. *Die Berufstruktur der Rhein-Mainischen Bevölkerung*, Rhein-Mainischen Forschungen, Heft 2, 1929.
A. Weitzel. " Die raumverschiebende Auswirkung der Neugliederung in dem rheinfränkischen Wirtschaftsgebiet ", *Erde und Wirtschaft*, Heft 3, 1929–30.
W. Behrmann and O. Maull. *Rhein-Mainischer Atlas für Wirtschaft, Verwaltung und Unterricht*, Frankfurt-a-M., 1929.
W. Brosius. *Die Lebensmittelversorgungsgebiete der Stadt Frankfurt-am-Main*, Rhein-Mainische Forschungen, Heft 10, 1934.
F. Zahn. *Bayern und das Reich*, 2nd edition, Munich, 1925.
W. Hartke. *Das Arbeits- und Wohnortsgebiet im Rhein-Mainischen Lebensraum*, Rhein-Mainischen Forschungen, Heft 18, 1938.
W. Hüfner. *Wirtschaftliche Verflechtungen in Südwestdeutschland*, Zum Wirtschaftlichen Schicksal Europas, Arbeiten zur Deutschen Problematik, No. 3, ed. C. Brinkmann, Berlin, 1935.

CHAPTER VII : CENTRAL GERMANY

G. Aubin. *Entwicklung und Bedeutung der Mitteldeutschen Industrie*, Halberstadt, 1924.
G. Hennig. *Landesplanung mit besonderer Berücksichtigung des mitteldeutschen Industriebezirks*, Tübingen, 1930.
E. Hübener. *Die Neugliederung Mitteldeutschlands, Reich und Länder*, Stuttgart, 1929. Also *Zeit. f. Geopolitik*, 1931.
Mitteldeutschland auf dem Wege zur Einheit, Denkschrift über die Wirkung der innerstaatlichen Schranken, Im Auftrage d. Prov.-Ausschusses d. Prov. Sachsen, hrsg. von Landeshauptmann der Provinz Sachsen, Merseburg, 1927.
Atlas der Landesplanung im engeren mitteldeutschen Industriebezirk, 1932.
H. Thormann and E. Staab. *Der Mitteldeutsche Raum, seine natürlichen, geschichtlichen, und wirtschaftlichen Grenzen*, Merseburg, 1929.
R. Reinhard. *Mitteldeuschland*, Geographische Zeitschrift, XLIII, 1936.
A. Penck. *Der Grossgau im Herzen Deutschlands*, Veröff. Handelskammer, Leipzig, 1921.
E. Hübener. " Reichsreform und Mitteldeutschland ", *Zeit. f. Geopolitik*, 1931.
" Die Pendelwanderung im Mitteldeutschen Industriegebiet ", *Vierteljahrshefte zur Statistik des Deutschen Reiches*, 1931.
Leipzig und Mitteldeutschland, Ein Beitrag zur Neugliederung des Reiches, Denkschrift für Rat und Stadtverordnete zu Leipzig, 1928.
W. Hoffmann and Richter, *Mitteldeutschland, Das Neue Wirtschaftszentrum*, Berlin, 1925.
J. Müller. *Der Mitteldeutsche Industriebezirk*, Jena, 1927.
—— *Thüringen und seine Stellung in und zu Mitteldeutschland*, Weimar, 1929.

CHAPTER VIII : THE BALTIC PROVINCES

G. Braun and W. Hartnack. *Die preussische Provinz Pommern bei der Neueinteilung Deutschlands*, Geog. Ges. z. Greifswald, Gedenkheft zum 50 Jahrigen Bestehen, 1932.

J. V. FOLKERS. "Mecklenburg in der Neugliederung des Deutschen Reiches", *Zeit. f. Geopolitik*, 1931.

R. LÜTGENS. *Die deutschen Seehäfen, Deutsche Sammlung*, Reihe Geographie, Band 6, Karlsruhe, 1934.

Wirtschafts und Verkehrsgeographischer Atlas von Pommern, Stettin, 1934.

E. HINRICHS. *Die Ostseelösung für Schleswig-Holstein, Lübeck, Mecklenburg*, Rendsburg, 1931.

CHAPTER IX : BERLIN—BRANDENBURG

M. PFANNSCHMIDT. *Die Industriesiedlung in Berlin und in der Mark Brandenburg*, Akademic für Landesforschung und Reichsplanung, Berlin, 1937.

F. LEYDEN. *Gross Berlin, Geographie der Weltstadt*, Breslau, 1933.

M. HALBWACHS. "Gross Berlin, Grande Agglomération ou Grande Ville." *Annales d'Histoire Économique et Sociale*, Vol. VI, 1934, pp. 547–570.

CHAPTER X : SILESIA

P. DRISKE. *Der Wirtschaftsorganismus Gross-Breslau, Ein Beitrag zur Wirtschaftsgeographie der Groszstadt*, Zur Wirtschaftsgeographie des deutschen Ostens, Band 12, 1936.

W. VOLZ. *Schlesien im Rahmen der wirtschaftsgeographischen Lage Deutschlands*, Breslau, 1925.

R. HARTSHORNE. *Geographic and Political Boundaries in Upper Silesia*, Annals Association of American Geographers, XXIII, 1933.

W. GEISLER, *Wirtschafts- und verkehrsgeographischer Atlas von Schlesien*, Breslau, 1932.

INDEX

For Product Safety Concerns and Information please contact our EU
representative GPSR@taylorandfrancis.com
Taylor & Francis Verlag GmbH, Kaufingerstraße 24, 80331 München, Germany

*9 7 8 0 4 1 5 8 6 8 5 4 9 *